I Am Enough

Library and Archives Canada Cataloguing in Publication

Rondeau, Danielle, 1986-, author
    I am enough : one lawyer's epic journey to fill the void / Danielle Rondeau.

Issued in print and electronic formats.
ISBN 978-1-77141-161-5 (paperback).--ISBN 978-1-77141-162-2 (pdf)

    1. Rondeau, Danielle, 1986-. 2. Rondeau, Danielle, 1986---Mental health. 3. Lawyers--Canada--Biography. 4. Eating disorders--Patients--Canada--Biography. 5. Anxiety--Patients--Canada--Biography. 6. Insomniacs--Canada--Biography. I. Title.

KE416.R65A3 2016   340.092   C2016-901963-2   C2016-901964-0

I Am Enough

One lawyer's epic journey to fill the void

Danielle Rondeau

First Published in Canada 2016 by Influence Publishing

Copyright © 2016 by Danielle Rondeau

All rights reserved. No part of this publication may be reproduced, stored in or introduced into a retrieval system, or transmitted, in any form, or by any means (electronic, mechanical, photocopying, recording or otherwise) without the prior written permission of the publisher. This book is sold subject to the condition that it shall not, by way of trade or otherwise, be lent, resold, hired out, or otherwise circulated without the publisher's prior consent in any form of binding or cover other than that in which it is published and without a similar condition including this condition being imposed on the subsequent purchaser.

Editor: Nina Shoroplova
Proofreader: Sue Kehoe
Typeset: Greg Salisbury
Book Cover Inspiration: Monique Orieux
Book Cover Design: Marla Thompson
Portrait Photographer: Joel Highet, Bright Pix Media
　　　　　www.brightpixmedia.com

DISCLAIMER:
Readers of this publication agree that neither Danielle Rondeau, nor her publisher will be held responsible or liable for damages that may be alleged as resulting directly or indirectly from the use of this publication. Neither the publisher nor the author can be held accountable for the information provided by, or actions, resulting from, accessing these resources.

Testimonials

"Danielle writes a poignant, raw, and emotional tale of her journey to self-love and self-acceptance. It's relatable, compelling, and worth the read!"
– Shannon Lagasse, health coach, founder of Hunger for Happiness, and author of *Why Can't You Just Eat?: A Look Inside the Mind of Anorexia, Bulimia and Binge Eating Disorder*

"The elusive and tumultuous journey to finding one's true passion; Danielle Rondeau's memoir is a powerful personal story of a young woman's path to self-development and discovery. Written with vulnerability and courage, Danielle opens up on her transformative journey spanning various careers, relationships, breakdowns, breakthroughs, and life in multiple cities. This book is an invaluable resource for anyone who is feeling lost or inauthentic, or anyone wanting to understand themselves and their own patterns of relating."
– Melissa James, speech-language pathologist and founder of Well Said: Toronto Speech Clinic

"Danielle's book is a gripping tale about the journey from surviving life to living into a place of abundant love. It is a call to each of us to step out from the darkness hidden in the comfort of *fine*, and into a world where deep, self-acceptance is available in every moment. A provocative and compelling ride—Danielle's brilliance is present throughout. Read this book."
– Adam Quiney, co-founder of Evergrowth Coaching

"Amazing story! I really had some aha moments that resonated with Danielle Rondeau's journey. It was so inspiring, there is a light at the end of the tunnel; you just need to keep your eyes open. Thank you!"

– Jennifer Demare, swine health professionals, veterinarian

"Danielle Rondeau shows beautifully what it means to be a seeker; creating awareness, letting it do its thing, being taken for a ride, and spit back out in a new place. In her writing she connects us to the courage it takes to embrace the ride and to the trust that our inner voice knows best —especially if it tells us that we are enough."

– Alice Smith, creative designer and founder of Alice Karolina

Acknowledgements

To James Killam, Q.C. of Killam Cordell Murray (KCM), the judges I clerked for, and all the other mentors in my life: thank you for always making time for me in schedules that were overflowing; for giving me a place to clear my head when I was completely caught inside it; for telling me stories about lives so rich I decided to go out and live my own; and for modelling what it means to serve others, to hold brilliance with humility, and to treat every human being with respect.

To Scott: thank you for sharing with me your wisdom and your grace; for getting me in touch with my body and reminding me how to love it; for cracking my heart open so wide I can no longer close it; and for showing me what it means to be connected at the soul.

To Dave: thank you for offering me more love and forgiveness than I ever deserved; for selflessly supporting me; for sharing with me your incredible family; and for weaving into every conversation a good and funny rant.

To Rachelle (Bay) LeBlanc Quiney, coach extraordinaire: thank you for being my trusty sounding board through years of ups and downs and ups that looked (to me in the moment) like downs, and for always, always (always!) holding for me a safe space, a fierce stand, and an overflowing bucket of love.

To Sarah Kalil: thank you for being the inspiration I didn't know I needed when I needed it the most; and for showing me that lawyers can be not only happy, but brilliant coaches, leaders, film producers, creators, storytellers, and bright shining spirits of light and love.

To my KCM family: thank you for letting me be myself—passionate about my side projects and new business ventures, overenthusiastic Christmas decorations included; for believing in me; and for having hearts big enough to take me in, let me go, and welcome me back.

To Steph—friend, soul sister, graceful wild woman: thank you for being with me through it all. I am ever grateful to Ester (may she rest in peace) and one fateful drive to Seattle at the crack of dawn.

To my brilliant sister: thank you for loving me through the rollercoaster; for hundreds of Skype conversations; and for, no matter how many clouds I got my head stuck in, always bringing me back to earth.

To my parents: thank you for making me me, and for loving me so much I couldn't help but stay that way. You taught me all the right lessons at exactly the right time and let me go when I needed to learn more on my own.

To the best brother anyone could have: thank you for pranking with me; for reading my mind; for letting me be your big sister; and for, at every turn, being respectful and kind. You remind me how to dream and how to be silly.

To my spiritual teachers: thank you for endless love and compassion; for sharing your wisdom with generosity; and for always showing up at just the right time.

To all of my friends who are really too good to be true: thank you for sharing this life with me, and for teaching me in your own way about truth, love, and laughter.

To my Accomplishment Coaching leader team, Accomplishment Coaching participant team, and Van City Coach Crew: thank you for transformation, love, and power.

To my high-school English teacher: thank you for helping me to remember through high-school dramas, first loves, and many other distractions, that I am a writer.

To everyone who lent me a home or a warm hug and a guiding conversation through the fog: thank you for teaching me surrender and trust.

To my writing buddy Zelius: thank you for many a philosophical debate and a good laugh; and for being part of the sweat and blood that made this happen.

To my Influence Publishing team—Julie Salisbury, Nina Shoroplova, and Lisa Halpern: thank you for extending deadlines, ears, and brilliant suggestions; for letting me rewrite this book over and over (and over); and for refusing to let me quit.

To Elizabeth Gilbert, Cheryl Strayed, Amy Poehler and every woman who has had the courage to tell her story: thank you for being the inspiration I needed in those moments when I'd forgotten why I started writing this book in the first place.

And to you, dear human: thank you for reading my story, and for being who you are in yours.

Contents

Testimonials V
Acknowledgements VII
Introduction XIII

Chapter 1—The Dark and the Light 1
Chapter 2—The End of "Fine" 17
Chapter 3—The Beginning of a Journey 25
Chapter 4—Asking for Help 43
Chapter 5—First Taste of Entrepreneurship 51
Chapter 6—Tending to the Fire 61
Chapter 7—The War on Goals 79
Chapter 8—Body Love 97
Chapter 9—A Sprinkle of Joy 109
Chapter 10—The Big Guns 115
Chapter 11—The Significance of Time 125
Chapter 12—Owning What I Want 135
Chapter 13—Something Greater 147
Chapter 14—Wild Love 163
Chapter 15—Bring on the Dark Side 175
Chapter 16—The Birth of a Warrior 195
Chapter 17—Surrender and Letting Go 209
Chapter 18—Death of a Journey 229
Chapter 19—The Hero's Return 235

Epilogue 241
Author Biography... 247
More About The Author 248

Introduction

This book is a memoir. It is a remembering and telling of the story of my epic three-year journey to find fulfillment and peace in my chaotic, addicted, stressed-out, fast-paced, never-good-enough, people-pleasing, approval-seeking internal world.

This book is also a love story. It is the story of my falling madly and deeply in love with various people, ideas, and things. And as much as it is about love, it is also about heartbreak. You will find entwined in these pages the story of my devastation when I realized again and again that each of the things I had fallen for were not mine and would not be the thing that would save me.

This book is also a dramatic adventure story. It is the story of my quest for everything; my quest for *my* everything. I believed with everything I had that it was out there—that answer; that truth; that magical thing. And I wanted it desperately. I set out to find it, falling in love fast and hard, giving new beliefs and pathways power. But the head-over-heels-this-is-my-everything feeling just wouldn't last. And so, I tore down new path after new path and set out for my truth, my magic, my everything, again. This pattern just happened to be the perfect recipe for drama and adventure.

On some level, I knew that my pattern was flawed and that there was another way to relate to the world—one where I could trust myself to have the answers I needed instead of looking for truth and validation from the outside—but I didn't know how to access it. Which brings me to the most important thing that this book is, and that is: a story of creation.

At its core, this story is about the creation of a belief system for myself that is mine. My entire journey has flowed from a deep-set commitment to reorganize my internal world so I could stop striving, people-pleasing, and avoiding my life, and be at peace in the moment. This necessitated a messy process of deconstructing my belief system and trying on new and different perspectives and paths.

It also necessitated reconstruction. And so began the biggest construction project I have ever undertaken. Day by day, brick by brick, I began building an internal foundation of self-love and acceptance; one that would allow me to live from my own truth, instead of looking for answers from others. I now have that foundation. I have also built on some solid walls, a leak-proof roof, heated floors, a fireplace, and a piano. And I will continue to toil away building my self-love empire—adding spare rooms and a garden, and one day a log beach house with a writer's loft and a massive claw-foot bathtub.

I say all this because while my inner world has undergone a complete restructuring and my default is no longer to relate to the world and others from being broken and not good enough, I have written most of this book from my old lens: a lens of seeking approval and answers from the world. I have done this because it gives a more accurate picture of my inner world and how I related to others around me at the relevant time in the story. But what this also means is that while the events and conversations in this book are true recollections of my experiences, they are not necessarily objectively accurate.

I do not profess to speak for anyone else. My writings about the words others have shared with me are not their truth. The people I have written into this book have their own beliefs. They are on their own paths. I have not told their story as it is not my place to do so. Nor have I tried to paint a full and accurate picture of the day-to-day events in my relationships, careers, and the other activities in my life. What I have included are some select conversations and events I had throughout my three-year journey that inspired me in some meaningful way, and that helped me to move forward with my personal mission.

In documenting the transformation of my internal world, I have tried to be as factually and temporally accurate as possible. I have referred to my journals, notes, blog posts, personal social media threads, texts, and emails. I have made alterations to my description of a few events and have changed some names of people for various reasons. Wherever I have made alterations, I have done so with the intention of staying true to my internal experience.

I am grateful for each and every person and circumstance I encountered along the way. Each has been a necessary part of my journey, right down to the last moments of writing this book.

I started writing this book mainly for that reason: it was a necessary part of my journey of transformation; a way of processing, letting go, and starting afresh on a new journey. But writing this book turned out to be so much more, including living the answer I had for so long been seeking.

I will do my best to explain how that came about, but first, "The Dark Side."

Chapter 1—The Dark and the Light

The Dark Side

Dread poured over me as a tiny rectangular box appeared in the bottom right-hand corner of my computer screen. It was a new email from one of the senior lawyers I was working for. I couldn't handle another assignment right now. I moved the mouse to the corner of my screen and clicked the message open. A red exclamation mark near the subject line indicated it was urgent. I held my breath as I took in the words: one brief sentence demanded to know where the application materials were that I was supposed to have prepared. My stomach lurched violently. I read the email once more, willing the words to be different. My stomach reeled again.

"What application did he mean?"

I had no idea. I didn't even recognize the name of the file. Panic set in as a buzz over my heart as I frantically riffled through the files in my office. I searched my emails. I looked the file up on the network. It was completely unfamiliar to me. I scanned my memory again and again. I had no recollection of talking to the partner about the file and no idea what application I was supposed to have prepared.

Rallying my courage, I sent a reply email to the partner asking what application he was referring to. When I didn't get a response immediately, I tried to focus on the million-and-one other tasks I had on my plate, hoping against hope that he would respond saying, "Oh, sorry about that; I sent the email to the wrong person."

Half an hour went by, then an hour, with no response. I didn't know what to do. It was completely possible I had forgotten. I was overwhelmed. I was billing ten to fifteen hours a day and six or so each day on the weekend. I had been for the past month and there was no light at the end of the tunnel. Instead, my to-do list seemed to double every day. I was exhausted. I had known articling at a large traditional law firm wouldn't be easy, but I had convinced myself I could handle it. I had armed myself with as much optimism and determination as I could, and had told myself that it was the best move for my legal career. I could do it; I would be fine.

"My fears were right," I thought. "I'm not cut out to be a lawyer. I have messed up something important. I will be fired. I'm incompetent. My life is over."

I stared at the mounds of paper on my desk and the boxes of documents creating a fortress all around me and fought back tears. "How will I ever get this all done? No wonder I am missing things!"

I felt defeated, alone, and ready to collapse into a sobbing mess. I couldn't have that. I would not cry at work. I needed to pull myself together. I slipped out to the bathroom and gave myself a stern pep talk.

"Okay, Danielle, look at the facts: you don't know for sure that you messed anything up. You haven't failed yet. You can still get everything done. The only way to be a failure in this situation is to give up. Now stop being so weak and emotional and get back to work!"

My clever mixture of threats and encouragement worked; I was able to clear my head to a point where I didn't have to actively fight back tears. After a quick makeup check I returned to my office, ready to battle my to-do list. But instead I found myself ambushed with a fresh attack. There were two more files on my chair. The top one had no note. The bottom one had a sticky that said, "Urgent."

"Great. Just great," I thought.

I took a deep breath, told myself it was okay, and took a

Chapter 1

closer look at the "Urgent" file—it was *that* file. The one I was supposed to have prepared the application on. I was just getting it now! I hadn't forgotten. I really had never seen it before.

I checked my email. There was no response from the partner. No missed calls. No apology. No acknowledgement that I was just receiving the file today. No acceptance of responsibility whatsoever. Just that one sticky note message—"Urgent."

Anger. Frustration. Betrayal. Helplessness. Emotions swirled in my gut.

Just then, one of the other articling students walked in and asked if I wanted to grab a coffee. I looked up and tried to respond but all that came were tears. The emotions I had been holding in for weeks could no longer be restrained. I explained the situation through my tears and received a hug. He suggested I go and speak with the partner who was head of the articling student committee about how overwhelmed I was feeling.

After making a second attempt to compose myself, that's exactly what I did. I explained how overwhelmed I was feeling, how exhausted I was, and how afraid I was that I was going to mess something up. The response I received was not all that helpful. Not that he didn't understand. He did. And he really did care. The problem was that he understood it all too well. He told me that even at his level (he had recently made partner) he often felt overwhelmed and often ended up working too much. He advised me to go and talk to the individual partners I worked for and ask to be given less work if I felt I *really* had too much on my plate.

Deep down I had known this was the answer I would get—a little sympathy, an "I'm in the same boat," and a "That's just the way it is."

I sighed, thanked the partner for listening, and left feeling nearly as helpless as I had felt when I entered, disheartened at the thought that it didn't really get much better, even in partnership.

Letting go of the hope that there might be a way for my work to be easier, I let my anxiety take over and fuel the fire I would need to make it through the day. I spent the afternoon drafting the urgent application, while everything else piled up, working late into the evening, and ending the night with a half-hearted attempt to organize myself for tomorrow.

It was just after midnight as I stepped out the front door of my office building onto snow-covered ground, steeling myself for the solitary five-block walk home. The frigid air cut my lungs like a cluster of tiny shards of glass as I attempted to adjust to breathing in temperatures hovering around minus forty degrees Celsius. It was the middle of January 2012 in Winnipeg, Manitoba, a city renowned for its unforgivingly long and bitterly cold winters. Steeling myself against the wind, I pulled my scarf up higher over my face and set out; the sound of snow crunching under my boots echoing eerily into the deserted street with each step.

"You should have called a cab," I chided myself a block later, as my mind came alive with vivid imagery of the risks of walking alone in downtown Winnipeg at that time of night, even on a weekday. It seemed the local news reported a stabbing or a body found in an alley every morning. I picked up my pace.

"It's only a few more blocks. You will be fine," I told myself.

I took a deep breath. My mind began to distract me with its usual subjects: the awful day I had had; the long list of things left unfinished on my desk; the rush of the indulgent escape I was onto next.

Suddenly, my skin began prickling. Senses alert, my eyes darted furiously around me scanning the deserted street. Half a block in front of me a man stepped out from an alley and

Chapter 1

began walking toward me on the sidewalk. He stumbled a little to the right and then to the left as he approached, clearly under the effects of some intoxicating substance. His clothes were dirty and torn, his jacket hanging open and falling half off one shoulder, the biting wind rippling the fabric of his thin shirt.

My heart began racing.

"He's not going to harm you. He's merely walking home too." I tried to reassure myself.

"He likely doesn't even have a home," another voice chimed in.

For a moment my heart broke as I imagined what his life might be like; but seconds later the violent images my mind had been producing returned. I contemplated running across the street to avoid him, but I didn't want to draw attention to myself. He seemed not to have noticed me so far. I decided it was better to just keep walking on my path, keep staying close to the curb ready to bolt if necessary, and keep hoping I would be fine.

"He's probably just drunk and wandering," I repeated in my head. Some have called me naïve, but I want to believe the best in people.

I held my breath. He stumbled a little toward me as we passed and looked up, glassy eyes half focusing slightly below my chin.

"Preddy lady," he said.

My heart shot up my throat. I began speed walking past him, breaking into a run even though I sensed he was not following me. When I stopped to look over my shoulder a block later, I could see him still stumbling along in the opposite direction, our passing completely forgotten. I breathed out the breath I had been holding. I was fine, but shaken. Adrenaline coursing through me, I jogged another block, looking over my shoulder every few seconds until I found myself once again on deserted streets.

I was nearly home. But that's not where I was going quite

yet. I had had a rough day, and now this. My heart was racing more than usual. I would never sleep. I was in need of comfort; something to ease this restless buzzing in my chest. I walked a block past my apartment building toward the light of the little convenience store—the only place open at this hour of the night—my mind easing its never-ending worrying as it began to anticipate what was ahead.

"What will I get this time?" a mischievous voice asked, as mouth-watering images of thick decadent milkshakes, saucy deep-dish pizza, and warm chocolate-chip banana bread came alive in my head.

Pulling myself from my decadent reverie, I found myself standing over the freezer staring at my reliable comfort food: a dozen different flavours of ice cream stared back.

"Oreo. Definitely."

I grabbed a two-litre tub out of the deep freeze and wandered through the remaining aisles of the store in case something else caught my eye. I stopped for a moment in front of the refrigerator and picked up a jug of chocolate milk. "Hmm, maybe with a bag of cookies," I thought.

"You can't have both," I reminded myself. "You have to be at work tomorrow, early, and that would take all night."

I sighed as I put the chocolate milk I had been holding back into the refrigerator and picked up a zero-calorie vitamin water. I would need that later. At the till, my eyes were drawn toward the chocolate bars on display for that purpose. I grabbed two, a KitKat and an Aero, and then with the justification of "I've had a really hard day," I grabbed a Coffee Crisp too.

I paid quickly, not making eye contact with the teller, as if by maintaining my own blindness I could go on unseen in my secret world. I was all set.

Arriving at my apartment five minutes later, two out of the

Chapter 1

three chocolate bars already consumed on my walk home, I quietly snuck into my room and pulled out my remaining treasures. I opened the tub of ice cream easily with my fingers—I'd learned to stretch the plastic wrapping around the lid so I could slide it off without using a knife—and dug in, scooping a large chunk of ice cream and cookie up with my fingers and putting it into my mouth.

"Ahhhh," I sighed.

I could feel the tension slowly easing from my shoulders, my mind quieting as it focused on its task. Another mouthful and then another filled the void, before I broke away from my love affair to go into the kitchen.

I returned with a spoon and a glass of red wine. After a few more hurried mouthfuls, I took a sip of wine and pulled out the half-finished painting I was working on and put it out on my desk with my paints, as if to convince myself that I was simply having a glass of wine and painting. As I picked up a paintbrush, my mind began reminding me of my to-do list and replaying the horrible day I had had, the whole scene screeching through my mind like old yellowing fingernails on a chalkboard.

"This can't be your life," a small, disgusted voice whispered. I could feel the black claws of depression threatening to pull me under.

"No, I will not give up!"

Justifying my escape, I dropped the paintbrush I was clutching suspended mid-stroke, took a huge gulp of wine, and returned to my ice cream.

Finishing the entire tub without stopping and feeling ready to burst, I forced myself to eat the Aero bar too, which I had saved for last because I knew that it would be the hardest to get rid of. The other bars had wafers that would get soaked in ice cream making them easier to get back up my throat and out of my body. The pure chocolate would simply stick in the bottom of my stomach. I could not afford those extra calories. I felt a small measure of pride at my strategy. I had been doing this for over seven years. I was an expert.

Making my way to the bathroom, I tied my hair back, turned the water on so that on the off-chance my roommate was awake she would not hear, lowered my face over the toilet, and put my fingers down my throat. I made sure I could see all of what I had eaten make its way into the toilet. I knew it would not be too challenging: ice cream comes up the easiest. At the first taste of stomach acid, I stopped. I used to go further to make sure I removed as many of the calories as possible, but these days I could not stand the heartburn. It made it even harder for me to fall asleep. I could not afford those sleepless hours when I had this much work.

Five minutes later, my throat raw and my stomach empty, I was exhausted. I drank the full bottle of zero calorie vitamin water I had purchased to prevent dehydration and replenish some of the nutrients I had vomited, and then chewed two Tums® to boost my calcium and ease any heartburn that would come. I brushed my teeth thoroughly to minimize corrosion from the stomach acid, and made my way to bed. Turning to my bedside clock, I saw the time was 2:20 a.m. I sighed and flipped the switch turning on my alarm, which was set to ring less than four hours later. Present to the looming heartburn, the dull ache in my abdomen, and the rawness of my tongue and esophagus, I curled into the fetal position and sank into a ball of shame, tears silently spilling through my lashes and soaking my pillow. It was an hour before exhaustion won over, allowing me to fall asleep.

Three hours later I was jarred awake by the foghorn that was my alarm. I woke to the same shame and self-hatred I'd curled up with. My body desperately longed to call in sick and go back to sleep, but awareness of the mountain of work I had to deal with was already taking control over my body. Anxiety was building the stores of adrenaline I would need to tackle the day, and I knew I would not fall back asleep even if I tried. I forced myself to sit up for a second before curling back into a ball, fresh tears spilling down my cheeks.

"If you stay home you will probably spend the day feeling awful about yourself, eating more food, throwing it up, feeling more self-hatred with each purge, and creating more anxiety about what you are not getting done," my mind warned.

It was true. I could not trust myself to rest when I was in this state. I forced myself to gather all the positive energy I could summon and jumped out of bed.

Before my feet could even hit the floor my survival strategy of forced optimism had taken over completely. My mind began planning all the things I would get done at work, the friend I would make time to catch up with over lunch, the trip to the gym I would fit in, how little food I would eat to make up for last night's binge, and how early I would get to bed to catch up on my sleep, feeding me promises that today I would be better; today I would be disciplined; today would go exactly as I planned: perfectly.

The Light Side

Six months earlier: Vancouver

Warm sunlight hit my cheek as my eyes flitted open to take in the beautiful vaulted ceiling high above my head. The rain had stopped. I smiled and turned over onto my side to check my bedside clock: 8:10 a.m. I smiled even bigger. I had been asleep for over eight hours! No wonder I felt so good. I stretched slowly to the right, then the left, ending in a full spread eagle. I felt *so* good.

My eye caught the navy and teal party dress hung on my closet door, reminding me what day it was. I couldn't believe I would be leaving this city so soon. I scanned the room that had been my home for the past eleven months, taking in each object with a mixture of sadness and love. To my right my wobbly wooden bedside table carried a Kleenex box, a couple of pens, an old notepad that read Robson Hall Faculty of Law, and my trusty foghorn alarm. Propping myself on an elbow I took in the wall to my right where a corkboard overflowed with pictures of my family and friends from Manitoba, and my recent outings with friends in Vancouver. Below the corkboard my cell phone sat charging among some papers on an old second-hand desk, a desk that housed many treasures—colourful markers, craft supplies, journals, and stacks of photos; and a dozen neatly organized file folders with labels like "Cellphone," "Clerking," "Taxes," "Articling Applications," and "Fun Things to Do in Vancouver." My eyes moved to the comfy swivel chair twirled slightly to the right in front of my desk, revealing the leather briefcase filled with highlighted case law, legal notepaper, and pens that I had casually dropped on its seat on returning home from work the evening before.

To my left, sunlight caught the glittering gems of the many trinkets and accessories that I had collected on thrift-store-scavenging adventures with friends and that now lined the window ledge spanning half the length of the room. To the right of the window a full length mirror, stately and tall, was strung with jewellery. Straight in front of me my closet doors were spread wide open, bursting forth a sweeping collection

Chapter 1

of garments—dark pencil skirts, blouses and blazers; spandex yoga wear, headbands, and running gear; glittering halter tops and miniskirts; wild bohemian pants and short-sleeved crops; leather jackets, oversized sunglasses, and caps with feathers; beachwear and cut off shorts; vibrantly coloured umbrellas and striped rubber boots; a Dr. Seuss "Thing One and Thing Two" Halloween costume my roommate and I had created and adorned; plain jeans, t-shirts, and hoodies; a winter coat, fur toque, and Winnipeg Jets jersey—and a mountain of every style of shoe.

In the far back corner of my room rested my latest creation, ripe for the tasting: thirty litres of homemade red wine. My body filled with excitement for the day ahead.

Just then my phone buzzed indicating I had received a text message. I rolled over and bounced out of bed, adding in a twirl and sliding across the hardwood floor towards my phone like a rock star.

"I'm so excited for the party tonight! What should I bring?"

It was one of my closest friends. I texted a reply with a few different options for items she might bring for the potluck, some happy faces, and exclamation marks, and then bounded into the kitchen feeling increasingly giddy. The delicious smell of freshly brewed coffee filled my nostrils. My roommate had already made coffee!

I made myself a piece of toast with peanut butter and banana, and sat down with my cup of coffee and the list I had made the day before of everything that needed to be organized for my goodbye party later that evening.

In a few days I would be moving back to my home province of Manitoba to complete my articles at one of the biggest law firms in downtown Winnipeg. Although I was sad to be leaving my friends in Vancouver, I was excited that I would be articling at such a prestigious firm. I smiled as I remembered how I'd been utterly dazzled the first time I'd attended a glamorous wine and cheese reception at a big law firm. Sipping on fine wine, staring out at city lights through floor-to-ceiling windows forty storeys in the air, my heart had stopped right in my chest.

I hadn't always been a city girl. Far from it. I had grown up on a hog farm in rural Manitoba. There I'd played in backyards and bushes, and helped out on the farm for the first eighteen years of my life. My idea of drinking fine wine had been to purchase wine in a glass bottle instead of a box. I had had a simple childhood, but one where I had always been encouraged to excel, to become independent, and to pursue a career less risky than farming, such as law or medicine. I had graduated the valedictorian of my thirteen-person high school class and moved to Winnipeg, completing my undergraduate degree in Psychology and Philosophy and following that with three years at Robson Hall Faculty of Law at the University of Manitoba.

I had had a loving family, good friends, and a high school sweetheart I was head over heels for in the farming community where I grew up, but as I made my way through university, the excitement and anonymity of the big city had begun calling to me in my dreams.

Although I had driven the two hours back to the country to visit my boyfriend and family nearly every weekend, by the time I was in my second year of law school, city life had begun to feel like *my* life. Graduating from law school at twenty-three in the spring of 2010, I had excitedly accepted a coveted position at the British Columbia Court of Appeal clerking for two Justices of the Court, and prepared to move to an even bigger city, Vancouver. I had begun work in September and it was now July 2011; my eleven-month clerkship term was complete.

In many ways these past months had been the happiest of

Chapter 1

my life, at least as far back as I could remember. I had worked on some fascinating legal cases and developed wonderful mentorship relationships with both the judges I was clerking for. I had made some amazing friends and enjoyed many a beautiful hike, a delicious meal, and an entertaining costume party. I had met and begun a relationship with a man named Dave who had a heart of gold. I had run my first half marathon at a pace that satisfied even my own high standards. I had walked to and from work at the Courthouse every day over the Granville Street Bridge, staring up at the mountains that stand majestic and tall to the north of Vancouver and out at the Pacific Ocean that spans to the west. There were moments of heaven; days even.

Today was turning into one of those days. My phone buzzed again on the table beside me as I finished my coffee and began cutting up an extensive variety of fresh fruit. The message was a flurry of excited questions from another friend. I responded with an equal amount of excitement and flipped open my laptop to turn on some music. Music blaring, I danced my way into my bedroom and returned dragging my giant tub of homemade red wine into the kitchen. After mixing in the entire mountain of fresh fruit I'd cut up plus a forty-ounce bottle of brandy, and taking a small taste test, my task was complete. Tonight we would celebrate with delicious sangria!

Feeling the buzz of excitement growing in the air and in my heart, I couldn't sit still. I decided to go for a run. I quickly changed and pulled on my running shoes and headed out into the late morning sun. As my feet raced along the seawall, the movement felt effortless, like my heart had flown out ahead of me and was pulling me forward. I was in love, drinking in every ounce of my surroundings, savouring each moment with the beautiful city I would soon be leaving.

As I ran, I began counting all the blessings my life had brought me so far. I had parents who loved me, a little brother I adored, and a brilliant sister with whom I would be travelling to Brazil in a few weeks. I couldn't wait! We would be visiting a good friend who had lived at my parents' farm as an exchange student during my grade eleven year.

I was grateful for all my travels. By the age of twenty-four, I had been to Europe twice, exploring nearly twenty different countries, once with close friends from law school for a two-month backpacking extravaganza, and once on a two-week solo expedition before beginning my clerkship. I had been to Disney World and to an all-inclusive resort in the Dominican Republic with my family. I had driven across Canada from Winnipeg to Vancouver through the Rockies, and from Winnipeg to Toronto through Chicago and Niagara Falls. I had ventured into the States bordering Manitoba and British Columbia (BC) many times for shopping and little outings, and had camped all over rural Manitoba.

I had friends from every period in my life—elementary school, high school, summer camp, undergraduate degree, law school, summer jobs, part-time jobs, travelling—many of whom I remained very close with. I had a massive extended family, with aunts and uncles and cousins and second cousins and two grandmas still living who loved me.

I was grateful that I had somehow managed to check my junk mail at exactly the right time, before it deleted the last-minute notice of an offer of a law clerk position in Vancouver. What an incredible year. I had gained two invaluable mentors, a fascinating behind-the-scenes experience at a courthouse, countless memories, and lifelong friends.

The gratitude and joy I felt was about to overtake me when a different voice tried to make itself heard. "What about all

Chapter 1

those other times?" it whispered. "Remember even two days ago, walking from coffee shop to coffee shop, filling yourself with calories and shame. You know how that ended."

But this time, love won. The voice faded away. Today, everything was perfect. My live-in demon could not ruin my mood. Love and gratitude overtook me and I couldn't help but break into a full-faced smile, joyfully skip-running back over the bridge toward home.

After lunch I went out to pick up a few last-minute things for the evening. On my return I passed a hair studio and, having a couple of hours to spare, spontaneously decided to get my hair done. I had an incredible conversation with the stylist about life as she cut, coloured, and styled my hair. I walked out of the studio a couple of hours later with a beautiful new do—a cute crop and a rich deep-brown colour—the perfect style and hue to make my eyes pop the moment I put on the party dress my roommate had lent me for the evening ahead. Every moment of the day was seamless.

The party turned out to be a smashing success. Throughout the evening our home filled with friends, food, drink, and laughter. At least thirty people dropped by. We were barbequing, playing games, laughing, drinking, eating, dancing, storytelling, doing tricks with apples and knives, adding extra vodka to the sangria, posing and taking pictures, and daring each other to drink a lot of milk—usual party etiquette. Everyone was enjoying themselves. I was beaming. I had only been living in this city for eleven months. I could not believe the amount of love that had gathered to see me off.

"Call two more cabs," someone was shouting in the living room through the laughter. "There are a lot of us!"

I smiled. The party was winding down and a group of us were heading out dancing. I was in the next room with a few close friends putting the final touches on my outfit. I had changed out of my party dress into a seventies leopard print onesie of my mother's and I looked hot! I had pulled out the shoulder pads, turned it into a mini skirt, and paired it with dangerously high silver heels, feather earrings, bright red lipstick, and a black felt hat, under which you could just see my massive smoky-blue eyes. One of my closest friends was beside me looking equally glamorous. We were posing for pictures and being silly, and getting ready for some serious dancing.

We finished tinkering with our outfits, our cabs arrived, and we set out. It was an epic night. I think someone at my party knew someone at the wedding afterparty we ended up at, although it may only have been the D.J. My best guess is the remaining wedding guests must have liked our outfits because they opened wide the doors to their little home in Strathcona and let us pour in and take over the dance floor. We danced our hearts out with two middle-aged aunts of the bride until after 4:00 a.m.

By the early morning both my feet and my heart had expanded to twice their normal size and felt like they would burst. As I fell into bed around the time the sun was coming up, I was filled with love. All I could think was, "How did my life get to be so awesome?" And "I can't believe we just crashed a wedding!" And "Wow, my feet hurt."

Chapter 2—The End of "Fine"

It was 11 p.m. on Sunday, January 6, 2013. I stood with my phone in my hand about to send a "See you then!" to my friend to confirm our 5:30 a.m. run the next morning. As I moved my finger toward the button, something stopped me from pushing send. There was nothing unusual about the message I was about to send; our rendezvous with running shoes before dawn was a tri-weekly occurrence, and had been for some time. But on this particular Sunday evening, there was a stirring of something deep inside that made me hesitate, finger hovering mid-motion, and pause.

I took a deep breath and closed my eyes to find my whole body screaming at me a question—one single word—"Why?"

"Why?" The question was accusing. It taunted me. It grew louder and louder, demanding an answer and refusing to slip quietly back into the darkness of the box it had burst from. What did it want, this frustrating word, *why*?

It raged on as I stood there, frozen, staring blankly at my phone.

"Why do you get up at dawn and rush off to work already feeling like you should have been there an hour earlier? Why do you arrive home late in the evening feeling like you didn't get enough done and should have stayed later? Why do you schedule runs at 5:30 in the morning despite only getting to bed at midnight? Why do you agree to social events in every spare minute? Why do you binge on unhealthy food no matter how hard you try to eat healthy and exercise right? Why do you only get four to six hours of sleep a night? Why can't you find the perfect guy? Why can't you be satisfied even when you do find the perfect guy? Why are you not content even though you have achieved the career you said you wanted? Why do you hate your to-do list? Why are you always overwhelmed? Why do you do all the things you do?"

"Why? Why? Why?"

My usual optimistic answers immediately popped into my head: "I do all these things because ... I like the challenge ... I like the excitement of the rush to meet a million deadlines ... it feels good to accomplish things ... I'm good at them ... people need me to ... I just like being busy, and ... well, at least for some of them, I just 'have to.' I have a great life. Everything is fine."

Visions of the past few months swirled through my head as I stood frozen by this question. Everything was fine, wasn't it?

A few weeks after the urgent file day in January 2012, I had returned to Vancouver for a weekend to celebrate the retirement of one of the judges I had clerked for. In the four days I was visiting, I had once again fallen head over heels in love with Vancouver. Feeling excitement bubble inside me as I contemplated life over drinks with a close friend, I had decided that this beautiful city would once again be home after articling.

Back in Winnipeg the remaining three months of my articles had become less painful; partly because my workload eased some and partly because I had something to look forward to: I had begun planning my move. I had decided I wanted to avoid what I labelled the "soul-sucking big law firms" and had immediately begun reaching out to everyone I knew in Vancouver who might have a lead on an opening at a small to mid-size litigation firm for a first-year associate.

Jobs were not the easiest to come by for young lawyers in the first year or two after being called to the Bar, especially in an attractive city like Vancouver. I had spoken with an advisor at a career counselling network who had told me that even though my resume was stellar, it would be extremely difficult, if not impossible, to land a position as a first-year associate in Vancouver. But everything about moving back had felt so right I could not be dissuaded. I had begun researching small firms and applying to all that interested me even if they were not advertising any openings. After most had returned with the responses of "Sorry, nothing available," or "Sorry, not now," and a few had not responded at all, I had begun to fear my career advisor was right—that it would be impossible for me to find a job in Vancouver without a few more years of experience. As a backup plan I had started applying to smaller litigation boutiques in Winnipeg, and had received a few offers. Just as I was about to accept one offer, I had been introduced by the second judge I had clerked for to a little Vancouver law firm which, at the time, had had no website or internet presence whatsoever, Killam Cordell Murray, Barristers & Solicitors (KCM). I had applied, and—all stars aligned—I had been hired!

After completing my articling term, and going on an extended vacation for most of May and June—four weeks on a safari in Western Africa, two weeks volunteering at an orphanage in Cape Town, and two weeks relaxing on the beach in Thailand—I had been ready to dive back into the law. And I had. When I had arrived in Vancouver in early July 2012, I had found myself thrown full time into a multimillion-dollar family-law dispute, which had been set for trial in the fall. It had been exciting. I fit right in at KCM, where laughter, pranks, and kindness were present even in the midst of busy times and hard work.

For the next six months, I had thrown myself into work and

other activities. I had reconnected with old friends, started running again, and resumed my romantic relationship with Dave. My life began turning out exactly the way I had wanted it to go. I had been able to check every box I had wanted to check. I should have felt grateful. And I did. I was grateful for the mentorship relationship that was beginning to form between me and James Killam, Q.C. I was grateful for the beautiful city that was once again my home, for my boyfriend, and for all of my friends.

Yet, I was always incredibly busy and still, at least a little (and often a lot), overwhelmed. Every moment of my time was filled with something. And, although I tried to ignore it, the void was still there. I had thought that coming back to Vancouver, working at a small law firm, being in a stable relationship, and reconnecting with friends would help me release my internal demon. But it persisted. I was still a perfectionist. I was still spending way more hours at work than a human should (not by demand of the partners, but by my own expectations). I was still sleeping only an average of four to six hours a night. I was still using food to cope with stress. I hated myself for not being able to lose the ten pounds I had gained during articling. I was still bingeing and purging three or four times a week, tormenting myself in the darkness of my own mind.

Despite the fullness of my schedule and my social life, I was lonely. No one knew my darkest secrets. Friends would comment on my twelve-hour workdays, my early morning runs, and the little sleep I ran my life on, and say, "I don't know how you do it!" Some friends in law would relate. We would complain together about the busyness, often in a boastful kind of way—"I haven't slept more than four hours a night in weeks! This case is going to kill me! I've been at the office since 6 a.m.—it's now 8 p.m. and I haven't left my desk!"

Chapter 2

Here and there, someone would seriously ask if I was okay. Occasionally I would acknowledge I was stressed, but more often than not I would cheerily respond that I was fine, and go on to list the amazing things in my life. And the truth is I believed it, mostly. I was *fine*.

That word was my saving grace and my captor. I was fine, no matter how many times I would push myself with running, social engagements, and work until I was so exhausted I would crack, stopping on the way home for a pizza, a bag of cookies and a jug of milk, or a tub of ice cream. I was fine, no matter how many times I would steal away into my room, devour the entire thing, and end with my face over the toilet. I was fine, no matter how many times I would curl up in bed, heart racing and full of shame. I was fine, no matter how many nights I lay awake hating myself for the pain I was putting myself through. I was fine, no matter how many times darkness won.

Without fail, I would wake up at the crack of dawn, heart racing, mind calculating how to fit in a million to-dos, smile spreading across my face, determined that today would be different. I convinced myself I was fine. Because I was fine I was stuck there, but it didn't matter because I was fine .

I had always been fine.

"No, I don't mind," I remember telling my mom when she suggested my younger-by-three-years sister begin taking figure skating lessons and participating in the other extracurriculars I was involved in a year sooner than I had started.

"It's fine that she's always better than me at everything."

"No, nothing's wrong. I'm just sick today," was my way to stay home from school in junior high to avoid watching friends who were no longer my friends become closer and closer with the louder, more popular group leader who had stepped in.

"Sure, I'll let you see my math homework. It's fine. I don't mind that you didn't invite me to your birthday and you stole my best friend."

"It's fine," I would say to the fourth giant homemade cookie that made its way to my tenth-grade brace-laced mouth as I felt my face begin to break out in hot red spots and my hips expand beyond the Barbie-like figure a few years earlier I was sure I would have forever.

"I don't care how I look. I don't care what you think. Don't you see my grunge pants and skull-faced hoodie that falls to my knees? Didn't you see my sixteen-year-old-self being all fun and crazy last weekend when I gave my romantic interest a bloody face after downing a few beers and jousting a beer bottle right into his chin? Didn't you hear me making jokes and running around the halls at 9:00 a.m. being silly after my second cup of coffee? Of course I'm fine. I only lie awake and cry myself to sleep sometimes. It's not so bad. I'm fine."

And it was true. I was always "fine." I always managed to stuff the pain down and summon my enthusiasm for life before venturing into the world. I was good at being fine. I had a lot of practice.

This time something was different, I could feel it.

I wasn't buying it. My old answers for why I did things were no longer satisfying. There had to be a bigger reason, a more important reason, for doing the things that I did other than simply the challenge of doing them and the rush of getting things done.

"Why?" The voice persisted.

I was stumped. It was early into the New Year and I had just come back from spending Christmas in Manitoba with my family. Over the holidays, I had had time to breathe and I had begun to see how the dark undercurrent of my life in Vancouver was not very different than it had been in Manitoba

Chapter 2

during articling, or as it had been in law school or undergrad, or high school before that.

The moment I stopped being busy I could feel the void was still there. And so, I had begun, as I always did when I hit the point of the new becoming the old, to look for things in my life I could change to solve the problem. I had begun thinking maybe I wasn't really satisfied with my romantic relationship, and maybe, I was working a little bit too much.

Even though I hadn't yet made any decisions about what to do about it, I had subconsciously started deconstructing my life. In the week since returning to Vancouver from Christmas in Manitoba I had ended things with Dave in a spectacularly drunken and ungraceful way, and work had naturally slowed since the trial that was set to go ahead had settled. Although neither change had happened in an ideal way, I thought at least the darkness in my life should be dissipating. Instead, it was worse. I felt disgusted with myself with how I had handled my breakup with Dave, and I was getting anxious with this lull at work.

And now I was standing here six days into the New Year with this "why?" question demanding to be answered. I stared blankly at my cell phone for another couple of minutes. And then it hit me. "I didn't have an answer." I didn't know why I did any of it.

My knees buckled and I sank into the chair behind me.

I let myself feel how scary that was. This was my life, and I wasn't running it. *It* was running me, and running me hard.

For the first time, I didn't—I couldn't—shove the feeling down, put the lid back on the box, turn back to my phone, push send, and distract myself by having a snack.

As I sat there feeling crushed by the weight of the awareness that I didn't know why I was living the life I was living, another thought came, quietly at first, and then with more conviction, filling my whole body. "I could choose something different."

I didn't have to be fine with fine. I finally admitted to myself what I knew deep down all along. It was not the fault of "soul-sucking big law firms" or the legal profession or the media or the expectations of others that left me feeling unfulfilled and exhausted, striving for some unattainable future that never arrived. I was the one who let *myself* off the hook from creating my life any differently.

I felt a new kind of peace emerge in that moment as I acknowledged that *fine* does not have to be how it goes, and that I wanted to create something that was different.

I looked back down at my phone and took the first bold step on what would become a three-year journey to fill that insatiable void in my life: I cancelled my 5:30 a.m. run with my friend. As I lay down to sleep fifteen minutes later, my heart had stopped racing. I knew I was no longer and would never again be fine with *fine*.

I didn't know where I was going next, but I was determined to make it mine.

Chapter 3—The Beginning of a Journey

Saying No, Again and Again

The delicious smells of carrot and ginger filled my nose as the spoon I was holding stopped midway to my mouth. I inhaled deeply, allowing myself to be filled with the savoury aromas. I brought the spoon to my lips and slowly took it into my mouth, relishing in the richness of the soup, before replacing the spoon to the bowl and turning back to my evening project. A notebook and several printed pages containing lists of questions I had found online were stacked on the table next to me. I had just finished making a list of the people I loved spending time with and why. I was on to the next question: What are fifteen activities you enjoyed in your childhood that you no longer participate in?

I smiled as I remembered my pre-teen self with a pad of paper and a pencil sitting out on the lawn at my parents' farm, sketching out in detail the twisting branches of the crab apple tree. They were few and far between, but I loved those quiet afternoons with a pad of paper and a tree.

I wrote down a few answers—drawing, figure skating, swimming, baseball, building tree forts, playing make-believe games, cards—and then paused to dip my crusty garlic bread into my soup. It was a little before 8:00 p.m. on a Wednesday evening in mid-January and I was enjoying a meal and my own company in a little café on Denman Street. I'd stumbled across the café by chance, and I was grateful. This soup was to die for! It was one of my favourites so far among the restaurants I'd walked into as if a natural part of the evening stroll I was increasingly finding myself taking.

I Am Enough

Although it had only been a few weeks, it seemed like months since that night I'd cancelled my early morning run. I barely recognized the calm, peaceful person sitting dipping buttery garlic bread into soup, not chastising herself for consuming the delicious calories, or for the unfinished legal work she had left on her desk. I thought back to that night, relishing the changes I'd made since. It was as if a stop had been pulled out and my entire life had begun flowing from that one little act.

For a start, I had been sleeping like I hadn't slept in years. For the past couple of weeks, six to eight hours of sleep had become the norm, instead of my usual four to six. The night I cancelled my run I had also turned off my alarm. When I woke up eight hours later I was still tired and, instead of jumping out of bed, I had let myself lie there for another hour. I knew the tiredness I was feeling was part of a bigger picture. I had been pushing myself so hard for so long to meet so many expectations that I no longer recognized the exhaustion as anything other than normal. Now that I had allowed myself to stop for a moment, I could feel how drained I was.

When I had risen that morning, I did something even more courageous. I texted my friend and cancelled all my 5:30 a.m. runs for the month. I cancelled a coffee with a friend and the yoga class I had planned to get myself to that evening. I mentally cancelled the billed nine-hour day I had expected to put in at work and replaced it with no expectations. Feeding off the high of having no expectations, I acknowledged that I needed an entire week for myself and cancelled all appointments for every other day that week, and then for the whole month. No yoga, no dinners, no runs, no visiting friends, no planning. No expectations. Not at work, not with respect to eating or exercising, nor being a good friend and family member. No plans and expectations for the entire month of January.

Chapter 3

The thought of having every morning, lunch, evening, and weekend completely free was exhilarating and it also terrified me. "How many people would I have to say no to? How many people would I disappoint? How would I fill my time?"

With respect to filling my time, I should not have worried. After a few evenings without a schedule I found myself drawn easily from one thing to the next—from Googling various ways to transform your life, to reading self-help books I came across, to wandering the beautiful city of Vancouver, to staring out at the ocean and enjoying long drawn-out meals at new restaurants. My time filled easily.

Tonight at the café, like most nights that I went wandering, I had brought along my journal and a little project related to filling the void I used to call "fine." Lately my activities had been focused on figuring out what I was passionate about. All the self-help literature I had been reading since embarking on this mission in the last two weeks had been telling me that filling your life with what you are passionate about is of central importance to creating a life that you *love*, instead of a life that is *fine*. So I was taking it on.

If you had asked me prior to January 2013 what I stood for or what I believed in, I would not have been able to give you an answer. Not a juicy one anyway. Maybe I would have said something generic like, "I believe in being kind to people," "helping others," or "finding happiness." But if you had probed a little further and asked what those things meant to me personally, and how I was going to make a difference, I would have been at a loss.

When I heard others talk passionately, I listened intently. I often agreed with what they were saying and even got passionate about their thing right along with them; but I didn't have my own steam. If truth be told, I wasn't really sure what was important to me. I did not have a bigger *why* or meaning for my life. I did not know what I was passionate about. I did not even know if I *was* passionate about something. I hadn't given myself permission to think about it, not since long before law school. I would say to myself, "What does it really matter? And who wants to be one of those crazy passionate people anyway?"

What I was realizing in these first few weeks of self-discovery was that secretly I was one of those crazy passionate people and I really did want to have a life fueled by passion, but I was scared. I was scared that if I looked I wouldn't find anything I could be passionate about, and that even if I did find something, I'd never be able to do it well enough or be lucky enough to make money at it, and I'd likely never make a difference anyway; I'd probably fail. So I had stopped looking. I didn't have big dreams that I cared deeply about, and I certainly didn't have a plan. I had picked what seemed like a good path and I was following it, hoping it was the right one and that I'd find fulfillment along the way.

It was time to take a stand for something, but for what? I looked back at the white lined paper beside me and an image flew through my mind. I was thirteen or fourteen and I was handing a red folder to my mother.

"This is for you," I had told her.

I couldn't remember whether the half-finished creation inside was meant as a gift, or whether I was making a request of her to keep it safe until I had time to finish it, but the feeling was one of pride and excitement. In that red folder was a rough, unfinished draft of my first novel.

"Writing," I thought. "Of course! I loved writing."

My favourite teacher in high school had been my English teacher, and I had gone to university wanting to become a writer or an English teacher or a professor myself. Somewhere along the way that dream had faded into the background and then been buried completely as I learned that the risks of not becoming a financially successful writer were such that it was much smarter to become a lawyer.

The next image that came to mind was a small hardcover book, rusty red with gold etching. I remembered ripping open the corrugated cardboard encasing to find the surprise gift that had arrived in the mail. Cracking open the hardcover, I had flipped through the pages to find my poem, tracing my finger over the lines of vivid imagery my younger, fourteen-year-old-self had captured for a Remembrance Day school project. Little had I known that my mother had sent it away a few years later, and that it would be accepted and published in an international book among the works of other poets.

"Writing. Poetry." I wrote the items down and took another spoonful of soup. I couldn't help but smile as a resonating feeling of *yes* filled my whole body.

As I wandered back to my apartment an hour later, I felt completely satisfied, and not simply as a result of consuming the delicious soup. I knew I was on the right path. I could feel it. Again I thought back over the past couple of weeks. I was pretty sure I hadn't really disappointed anyone with my nos, and the fear and anxiety I had had to overcome to clear this space for myself on my schedule had been completely worth it. There was a skip in my step as I made my way home.

"Maybe I will sign up for a painting class so I can paint some more trees," I thought.

The Courage to Be Seen

I picked up the phone and hit the speed dial labelled "Mom."

"It's going to be okay," I told myself. "She will still love you. She will understand." I felt a shiver crawl up my spine, the wet evening breeze settling into my bones, ignoring the layers I had wrapped around myself.

As her phone rang my pulse quickened. I looked up into the dimly lit alley behind my apartment building that I had ended up in after a few evening hours of wandering Vancouver in January drizzle, building up my courage to make this call.

"Perfect place for sharing secrets," I thought with a distant, echoing laugh.

"Hello." The warm voice of my mother greeted me from the other end of the line.

"Hi, Mom. It's me," I heard myself say, before falling into the electrified hush that surrounded me. She waited silently without going into her usual inquiries about my week, as if she could tell by the tenor of my voice that I had something important to say.

"I have to tell you something," I continued. The seconds ticked by at a snail's pace as I tried to find the words I knew I desperately needed to say. I was terrified. I didn't want her to think less of me or to blame herself for not being able to help me sooner, but I knew I had to stop hiding.

"Mom, I'm bulimic," I said with a quiet kind of pleading in my voice, silently willing her to understand.

"What do you mean?" she asked after a silent pause, although I sensed she already knew and was simply putting off the truth of what I had said for a moment longer.

"It means I sometimes eat a lot of food and then throw it up." I replied.

I couldn't stand the silence. I continued. "You remember in my first year of university when I lost all that weight? I wasn't eating enough. I was anorexic. It slowly turned into bulimia.

Chapter 3

I've had an eating disorder for about eight years."

I stopped. More silence. I could feel her pain through the phone. The electricity that had been coursing through my veins froze and settled into a tight clamp around my heart. I could never go back. All the dreams I had had of recovering in secret and never having to share this tormenting pain with anyone else were gone. Now my mom had to feel it too.

"I don't do it as much anymore," I spoke into the silence, trying to reassure her. "I'm getting better."

"Wow." Her faint, tear-choked words reached my ears. "I didn't know. Are you okay? I wish I had known. I wish I could have helped."

"I know. I'm okay." I replied. "I'm sorry."

We were both crying now. I was sorry. I was sorry I had hidden my secret for so long. I was sorry for all the pain I had caused. I was sorry for all my sneaking around and for my lies.

"I'm sorry. I just couldn't tell you. I didn't know how."

"It's okay," she said, after a few shaky deep breaths. "I just want you to know I love you very much. I'm always here for you if you need help."

"I love you too, Mom. I know. Can I talk to Dad?"

The conversation with my father was just as challenging. Although his response was less emotional, I knew my words had made their way past his strong, quiet exterior. I felt like I had just driven a stake into the hearts of both of my parents. I didn't want them to blame themselves. It wasn't their fault. I'd chosen my own path. I had desperately wanted to keep them from feeling the pain and worry I knew they would feel when I shared my secret. But something deep inside me knew that the only way I could recover would be if I could let go of the shame I held over myself for having an eating disorder. That meant being seen.

As I hung up the phone, although I was exhausted and still in some measure of pain, I felt lighter too. I had shared my secret and I was okay. My parents were still my parents. They still loved me. I was okay.

Over the next few days I began sharing my secret with a few close friends, each time steeling myself for rejection, and instead finding I was loved just as much as before. I left each interaction with a lighter heart and a deeper sense of being okay. My vulnerability muscle grew stronger and each new conversation became slightly easier than the last, until about a week later when I realized there was another conversation, I desperately needed to have.

"Okay, ready. Go!" I ripped my eyes from the beautiful twentieth-storey view outside my office window and propelled myself out of my chair. I made it halfway down the hall toward the office at its end before turning around and quickly returning to my chair.

"You have to do this," I told myself. "It's going to be okay. You have some money saved up. Working at a coffee shop won't be so bad. You don't even know if you want to do this lawyer thing anyway. You will find another job." My thoughts were drowned out by the beating of my heart.

I closed my door and began pacing back and forth continuing my pep talk to myself. "You can do this. You've been revealing your deepest secrets to people all week and you have not been struck by lightning yet." I reminded myself, "In fact, it has gone exceptionally well."

I tried to fill myself with the strength I'd found to have those conversations. "You can do this," I repeated to myself. "If you can tell your family and friends about your darkest struggles, surely you can have this conversation with your boss." I shook the gathering stress off my hands and made another attempt at

Chapter 3

walking the fifteen steps down the hall. This time I didn't even make it past the doorway of my own office.

I was beginning to get really frustrated at the extent of my own fear. I tried a different tactic with myself. "What's more important? Money or finding a way to fill this void?" I tried to remind myself of my priorities. But it wasn't the answer to that question that was stopping me.

Growing up on a farm where the weather and the market each have a big say in the size of your bank account, I had learned from my parents both how to be responsible with money and that money wasn't everything. My family had been through good years and bad, and we had always survived. Deep down I trusted I would be okay financially. No, it was something else that kept me glued to my chair like my life depended on it. I tried again to outsmart my fear, this time hitting the nerve on the head.

"What's more important," I asked myself, "making sure you don't disappoint someone, or finally finding a way to fill this void?"

Of course, it was my people-pleasing that was getting in the way. I was afraid of all the judgments I might be saddled with—failure, weak, just can't hack it, not good enough—the list went on and on. All these judgments were my own, but I thought that if I left law everyone else would secretly be labelling me too. No one would respect me. No one would like me. My worries about the interior workings of other people's minds were preventing me from having the conversation with my boss that I needed to have. And I really needed to have it. I could not focus. I was struggling with whether law was the right path for me. I was not as motivated at work as I had been. My productivity was sliding and the number of my billed hours was definitely sliding.

I had to tell him what was going on and offer to quit. I had come to the sensible conclusion the night before. "Better to choose it myself and be empowered about going to work in a coffee shop when I run out of money instead of waiting for them to fire me," I thought. "They will notice eventually, and then it will be worse."

The thought of that did it. With one last "You can do this," I forced myself out of my chair and speed-walked-ran down the hall, not stopping to even breathe until I was at James Killam's door.

"What are you doing? Stop! Go back!" I shouted silently at myself. But it was too late, the sound of my knuckles hitting the wood was already echoing down the hall. I was being welcomed in.

My mouth moved up and down a few times before I managed to get any sound to come out. "Can I talk to you about something?" I asked meekly.

"Of course," he replied, inviting me to close the door. Grateful for the privacy, I did, and then nervously sat down trying to figure out how to begin.

After a few moments the sentences started to flow, and then began tumbling out all at once. I wanted to be understood more than anything. And so I explained everything—my confusion about law as a career, my inability to focus at work, and my dwindling billed hours. I shared with him my struggles with bulimia. I explained that I had hit a breaking point with all of it and that I was trying to figure it out. He did not judge me or get angry, nor did he accept my offer to quit. Instead, for over two hours in the middle of the afternoon on a work day, he listened to everything I had to say and made me feel understood and accepted by sharing some stories of his own life and career path. By the end of our conversation he convinced me not to

Chapter 3

make any rash decisions. I did not need to go work at a coffee shop. I left his office with a part-time work arrangement that was acceptable to both of us, and some space in my schedule to focus on figuring out my passions and filling the void.

I was surprised by the response, although I should not have been. As was almost always the case, my overreactive catastrophizing internal critic ignored many important facts in determining how much sweat and heart pounding to dole out. By this point I already knew Jamie (as I had been invited to call him) was a kind person. I had been working closely with him for the past six months and he had become a friend and mentor. We had shared many laughs and I knew he cared about me.

I thought back with gratitude to that fateful Saturday in March 2012 when I had arrived at KCM for an interview. I had been dressed to the max in a suit, makeup, heels, and jewellery—and had walked into what felt not so much like a law office, but like a home. Jamie had sat in jeans and a sweater, feet propped up on his desk, a warm mischievous smile welcoming my nervous overdressed self into his office. The view of beautiful downtown Vancouver spanned one side of his desk; on the other, a couch with a stack of sheet music on one of its cushions, a guitar leaning casually on its stand, and Piper, a cute dishevelled little dog, curled up at its base. I had sat down in the chair opposite him taking in my surroundings in awe, wishing I would have worn something a little more comfortable.

As I began working, I learned that not only was Jamie an incredibly talented lawyer and invaluable mentor for my legal career, he was also kind, funny, and possessed a sense of integrity that commanded respect. The entire office exuded these values. I admired Jamie instantly, both as a lawyer and as a person. Fortunately for me, our relationship formed quite naturally as we both had the same playful, somewhat mischievous, sense of humour. My visits to his office to discuss a file often turned into conversations about life. We laughed and joked. He told stories. I listened. We laughed and joked some more. I loved it.

Still, I hadn't quite expected this. As I sat once again in my own office chair a few hours later, the reality of what had just happened began to sink in. "I'm still a lawyer! I still have a job! And it's part-time! I'm a part-time lawyer! I get to keep figuring out my passions, and I get to keep working at my law firm!"

I couldn't believe it. Something I had always thought was impossible was now my life.

A Vision That Was Mine

I took a sip of wine, shook my head, and laughed to myself as I pulled my eyes away from my laptop and looked out at the cityscape before me. I was settled down for an evening in. My roommates and good friends—a couple who were also lawyers—were out for the evening. I had been renting the spare room in their twenty-fifth floor downtown apartment since I had moved back to Vancouver the previous July. It was an arrangement that was initially planned to last six months, but had been working so well we had extended it. It was now late January, seven months in.

Watching the sun streak brilliant colours and sink its last breath of light into the ocean as the skyscrapers transformed into glittering jewels, my heart expanded in my chest. What a view! It seemed this city would never cease to take my breath away.

As my heart returned to its normal size and my eyes flitted back to my computer screen, I realized the thought I had

Chapter 3

chuckled at a few moments earlier had settled in to stay. "Actually, I could do that. Why not?"

Over the past month I had begun following a number of personal development bloggers on the internet, including Simon Sinek, Leo Babauta, and most recently, Scott Dinsmore[1]. It was Scott's blog—www.liveyourlegend.net—that had held me captive for the past hour as I consumed a number of his posts, and now, left me sitting with this thought. "I could do it. I could start a blog."

My little dates with myself over the past month had led me to the realization that I was actually passionate about a number of things. Writing and poetry were the beginning of a flood of ideas on how I might create a life I loved, while making a difference for others. I could facilitate events and workshops for lawyers, and maybe eventually I could create an online course or write a book!

As I began outing my dark secret and talking to other young lawyers about their experiences of law and life, I found that many had also used substances—alcohol, food, sex, shopping, or even drugs—to deal with stress and try to fill an insatiable void. Many believed as I had that in order to be successful, both stress and coping mechanisms were necessary: this was simply the way life was. A vivid memory of a conversation I had had with the other articling students during my articling year in Manitoba flooded my mind, reminding me of the severity of the issue.

"What I would do," I had said, "is keep a can of Comet in my drawer, and when I really can't take it anymore, I could just grab it and …." I had lifted my hand and made a motion of shaking Comet into my face while making whimpering noises.

---

[1] Scott Dinsmore died in September 2015. I send my condolences to his family and the Live Your Legend community, and my love and gratitude for the inspiration he was to me and thousands of others.

The others at the table had laughed.

"Wow, now that's creative," one of them had said.

We had been out for lunch on a Friday, and having just finishing our meal, had been enjoying the last of each other's company before gluing ourselves back in front of our computer screens. The topic of conversation had ranged from comparing work hours to complaining about work to joking about creative ways to do ourselves in. A typical lunch.

The seriousness of the conversation had entered our consciousness briefly when one of us had brought up the news story about an articling student in Toronto who it appeared had actually gone so far as to take her own life. The story was heartbreaking. We had each mumbled something about how awful it was that that could happen.

But it had been too close to home. We couldn't allow ourselves to dwell on it. Somebody had mentioned the weather. It had been a snowstorm outside. We had gone back to laughing.

I sighed at the memory. As much as I wanted and needed to figure out how to fill this void for my own sanity, I wanted to help others too. I also wanted to find a way to turn some of my passions into a business as I was starting to feel like I might not want to practise law forever, even on a part-time basis. I had been struggling with how to do it, and now it was starting to come together. A blog would be the perfect way to both process what I was going through and share what I was learning with other young lawyers. I was finding out from my research that many people had turned their blogs into successful businesses. In fact, I had just signed up for one of the courses offered on Live Your Legend called "How to Connect with Anyone." I could create a successful blog too.

Over the next weeks I set to work, bouncing ideas for blog names off a few friends and getting advice on the technical

Chapter 3

side of things from my new online community at Live Your Legend. Through a simple Google search, I came across a gold mine of a resource—www.howtomakemyblog.com—containing all the advice I needed on domain names, webhosting, and setting up a blogging platform. By mid-February, I had my own blog!

Next I sat down to write my first blog post summarizing the journey I had been on so far; which, after many rereads, an hour of hesitation, gathering up my courage, closing my eyes and clicking publish, went into the World Wide Web on February 25, 2013. A little over a month later, I had published over ten blog posts on my blog. I spent a lot of time getting clear on my growing mission and vision for the site and, to capture those more accurately, I changed its name from www.JJDLawConnection.com to www.TrashYourStress.com[2] (TYS). In early April 2013, I uploaded my vision and mission onto my new site.

About Trash Your Stress

The Trash Your Stress Vision—A Future without Stress

I envision a legal community where stress is discussed without stigma—one where young lawyers feel comfortable sharing the stresses in their lives and asking each other for help. I believe that the key to creating this type of community begins with open expression and encouragement of sharing in a more relaxed, fun setting rather than in traditional closed-door counselling. If we can sit across the table from each other and talk about stress and mental

---

[2] My Trash Your Stress blog posts are now located in the archives of my new site www.DanielleRondeau.com/archives.

health issues in meaningful ways, including brainstorming practical strategies to implement stress reduction in our lives, we could make leaps forward in the process of change. Young lawyers need to come together to solve these issues rather than feeling that we are alone or in competition with each other, or that by sharing our struggles we will be viewed as weak or that we will be taken advantage of. These myths need to be exposed for what they truly are: myths. The truth is that we all experience the stressful effects of this profession.

I've personally experienced how talking about these issues can be uncomfortable and how making changes can be scary, but I also know how important it is to deal with these things in order to finding happiness, balance, and meaning. Let's get together and create an inclusive community of young lawyers who are comfortable discussing stress-related issues so that we can go back into our firms and our lives and make some meaningful changes for ourselves and our profession.

The Trash Your Stress Mission

Let's Talk. Let's Make This Real.

Outline of Project

I am dedicated to getting rid of stress in the legal profession, with a focus on helping young lawyers not just to survive in this profession, but to actually love their lives and everything this profession has to offer. I envision this project making changes toward a legal profession in which lawyers are happy and healthy, and feel fulfilled in all areas of their lives.

Chapter 3

Objectives

- Raise awareness and reduce stigma associated with talking about stress and mental health issues by creating a community where young lawyers and law students can discuss these issues openly.
- Challenge stressful norms by empowering young lawyers to speak out and take control over their lives.
- Create a vehicle for personal change by offering each young lawyer access to a support network dedicated to thinking creatively about ways in which to get rid of stress in each of our individual lives.
- Create a vehicle for change in our profession by reaching out to senior members of the bar and bridging the generation gap.
- Take a prevention approach and raise awareness about stress and mental health issues in law schools.

Implementation

This blog supports these objectives. I write about the causes of stress, ways to overcome stress, and also of the experiences (both frustrating and inspiring) of young lawyers whom I have interviewed. I have met with a number of young lawyers both in informal chats and in more formal interview settings, and through this process have gathered information on the stressors that affect young lawyers as well as strategies to overcome these stressors.

From these discussions and my own experiences, I am in the process of creating some Stress-Busting Tools that young lawyers could use to reduce stress in their lives.

I also hope to use these experiences and ideas as the basis for topics of discussion at events I will host in the future for young lawyers and law students.

I Am Enough

How You Can Help

Please contact me if you are interested in participating in any way. Everyone has something valuable to share!
 I hope you will all join us and Trash Your Stress for good!

Chapter 4—Asking for Help

The Breaking Point

The darkness was immense, closing in, threatening to swallow me if I stopped. Rage coursed through me, propelling my body forward like the arms of a tantrum-throwing child. The pain was raw, primitive. I wanted to beat my chest and hurl things at the murky sky. The pain terrified me. I didn't know what to do with it. I felt the beginning of what was either a scream or a cry bubble up in my throat and threaten to escape. I pushed it down and ran harder—a safe release of the hatred I had been building up in a vicious case against myself. Every few moments, light flickered and gleamed off the wet sheen on the pavement as a car approached and passed by on the road beside me.

It was an evening in early May, although the gloomy cloud-covered sky releasing a slow continuous drizzle made it feel more like November. I was grateful for the rain and the gloom making my stormy disposition go unnoticed to those I tore past on the sidewalk as they walked by, eyes downcast, heads safely tucked under their umbrellas. I had been running at top speed for about ten minutes—through the streets, down to the water, along the seawall, onto the bridge—I barely noticed where my feet had taken me. I was in the middle of Granville Street Bridge, wind whipping my hair and taking my tears that I could no longer hold in down into the ocean with the rain, before I stopped and collapsed to the ground holding my knees.

"Why do you keep doing this to yourself?" I seethed into the darkness of my own mind. Two hours earlier I had arrived home, stressed, thinking about all the things I hadn't done at work and the blog post I still needed to write, trying to cajole myself into going to yoga even though deep down I knew I would never get there, and instead finding myself in the kitchen having devoured two Clif bars and my leftover pasta from the previous night before becoming conscious of what I was doing.

By that point, it was too late to stop.

I went out and bought some cookies and a litre of chocolate milk from the IGA on the corner and finished that off too, and then proceeded to try and remove all the contents of my stomach into the toilet.

I had been doing so well.

I had spent most of January and February uncovering my hidden passions, sharing dark secrets, and carving out more time for myself. In March and April, I had started reaching out to other young lawyers to connect, sometimes swapping battle tales, sometimes interviewing them and giving their stories an anonymous voice on my blog. TYS was starting to grow, to become something. I could feel it. Friends and acquaintances kept referring friends and acquaintances to me until I was meeting for coffee with a new face once or twice a week.

Not only was a small community beginning to form around TYS, but I was also gaining some awareness about this thing called stress, what was causing it, and what I might do to be proactive and reduce its presence in my life. The first realization and uncomfortable pill I had to swallow was that *I* was the one who was causing the majority of stress in my life, not others. It was my own unrealistic expectations for myself, my own catastrophizing of possible future scenarios that would likely never occur, and my own harsh internal critic repeating over and over that I was not good enough that created most of the anxiety in my life and the unhealthy coping mechanisms that came along with the anxiety.

Chapter 4

After admitting to myself that stress was not caused by not having enough time and bad luck, I set out finding ways to curb it. First, I tackled catastrophizing. Then, I started building in daily practices to make myself present to what was important to me, and to remind myself that no matter what I had done or not done during the day, it was enough; I was enough. As I went along, I wrote blog posts sharing the vital lessons I was learning.

I had thought that with discovering my passions, releasing my dark secrets, reducing my work hours, starting a blog, reaching out to other young lawyers, and tackling stress head-on, I would finally be able to quiet the demon inside my head. And I had for a time. For most of January my internal critic had remained silent as I became excited about the changes I was making and the passions I was discovering.

As February rolled around, however, even with all of the exciting things I was taking on, the voices started to return. Quietly at first, so that I continued to be convinced I could handle them, and then more persistently and viciously.

"You're not doing enough at work," turned into, "you're not blogging enough *and* you're not doing enough at work. And guess what? All that freedom you gave yourself to eat whatever you wanted in January—it made you fat. Now you have to lose those extra five pounds you've put on, too, on top of the ten you gained during articling."

It was a game I couldn't win. I would pick myself up for a few days with inspirational quotes or books and write a blog post about it, and just when I'd start thinking I'd solved the problem, I'd fall off again and the self-loathing would return. I wasn't bingeing and purging quite as often as before I'd started on this mission, but I still hadn't stopped. Every time my inner critic won and I'd gorged on something rich or thrown up my dinner, I'd lost a little more faith in myself and my ability to kick my bad habits and create a life I loved.

Now, four months in to this journey, crouched into a ball on a bridge in the dreary drizzle, I felt defeat. My tears fell furiously around me, blown by the wind. Every ounce of energy I had was directed in a venomous rage toward my own self. "Why can you never keep your own promises?" it thundered. "And why do you always convince yourself that you can?" I didn't know what to do.

Through my frustration I heard a voice deep within say, "You need some help."

I had heard that voice many times before but I had always refused to listen. Instead I would come up with some brilliant new strategy for overcoming my struggles, sure it would be the thing that would fix everything, and I would set out to do it, alone. When I would fail at implementing the strategy I'd collapse into despair for a day or two, until I found enough strength to go in search of the next one.

This time I'd had enough. It was time to admit what I did not want to admit. I could not do this alone. I never really had been alone of course—I had mentors and friends and family surrounding me my entire life—but I rarely asked for help. And when it came to rearranging the interior of my own mind, I never asked for help. It was only a few months ago that I'd worked up the courage to let those closest to me have a peek at what I was convinced was a serious mess going on in my head, never mind invite someone in to help me clean house.

"Okay, fine." I shouted into the dreary May air. "I won't do it alone." I watched water droplets roll off my iPhone as I pulled it out of my arm band and looked up the number of the woman who had shown me the possibility of another way. Without giving myself time to rethink the decision I quickly pulled myself together and dialed the number.

Chapter 4

"Hi Sarah, it's Danielle. I'm ready to sign up for some life coaching."

I had met Sarah Kalil around the time I started my blog back in February through an introduction made by my roommate who had continued to be incredibly supportive of me throughout this entire transition. Sarah was a lawyer-turned-film producer and life coach, a career combination I thought was incredibly cool. But the thing I was most blown away by was the positive energy she exuded—it seemed to fill up the entire room. At the time we had met I had had no idea what life coaching was, so I had taken her up on an offer of a sample coaching session by phone. By the end of that call, I had been excited and ready to hire her to help me move forward with my dreams. I believe my exact words were: "Yes, I am so frickin' ready!"

But by the next day I had retreated. I had convinced myself I couldn't possibly spend that much money on myself; I had been doing fine on my own; I changed my mind on signing up.

This time I knew my decision would stick. I secured my phone back into my arm band and began to jog home.

By the time I arrived back at my apartment, I was soaked, but I felt a million times lighter. I had a life coach! As much as I had been resistant to allowing someone to help me sort myself out, I knew I was moving in the right direction. Curled up in my room after a hot shower, I found that not only had I stopped beating myself up, but I had found the inspiration for the topic for my next series of blog posts: asking for help.

A Coach in My Corner

"I can't believe I actually did that," I thought. I had just walked to the garbage and thrown out the half-finished crumbly buttery blueberry scone that had been sitting in front of me on a white china plate. Not that I hadn't thrown out food before, but I couldn't remember a time when I had given in to my self-sabotaging habit and then stopped myself mid-binge and thrown out the food. I didn't like wasting, but I knew that if I kept it for later that would only be postponing an inevitable binge-and-purge session. The flaky baked goodness would torment me from whichever cupboard I put it in until I gave in and consumed it, likely along with a number of other forbidden sugary treats.

Turning back to the questions I was answering on my laptop, I felt proud of myself. Sarah had given me an exercise to help me get complete with how things had gone so far with ending my bulimia, feeling content with my weight and my body image, no longer comparing myself in an unhealthy way with beautiful, powerful women in my life and the media, and my envy of my younger sister whom I had always thought was perfect and who was taller and skinnier than me. From what I understood of completion, it was a coaching process intended to help me obtain closure with circumstances or people from the past and arrive at a more peaceful inner state. The exercise was inviting me to let go of all the feelings and lingering energy I was holding against myself and others, to take responsibility for how everything had gone so far in my recovery, and to access some gratitude for the progress I had made. I knew that from a place of peaceful acceptance and gratitude (instead of frustration and self-hate) it would be much easier to make progress on my goal to trash this bad habit forever.

As I answered the remaining questions I began to feel lighter. The exercise was reminding me of the power I always have to choose something different and giving me the motivation to do so. Another hour later I arrived at the last question, and wrote, "It is complete just as it is and just as it is not."

Chapter 4

I felt so much space around me. I had nowhere to rush off to, nothing that was in urgent need of my attention, and no feelings I wanted to numb with food. Even though I had just consumed a fatty latte and half a sugary scone, which would often trigger an uncontrollable urge to binge and purge, I felt at peace, just as it was, and just as it was not.

I couldn't believe it. I was so grateful. "Completion is really amazing," I thought. "Actually, life coaching is really amazing all around." I was getting so much out of my weekly conversations with Sarah. We had been coaching for about a month. In that time, we had come up with five words to describe my essence (the life force energy that is the core of who I am when I am uninhibited by fears and social conditioning), I had got clear on a big picture of how I wanted my life to look a few years from now, and I had created some projects to help bring my reality into alignment with that bigger picture vision. My five main objectives were to be free of bulimia, to start a Trash Your Stress revolution in the legal profession, to make enough money so that I could choose not to work as a lawyer if I did not want to, to start a local mastermind group, and to connect with a life partner.

All of these things were outside my comfort zone, and it was incredible to have someone to help me shift my fears out of the way and to keep me accountable every week for taking action on my projects. As I walked home, I thought about the completion exercise I had just taken on and the peace I now felt.

"I certainly would not have had access to something this powerful without coaching," I thought, "and it likely would have taken me a long time to accept how everything had gone and forgive myself this deeply."

With Sarah's encouragement and support, I had also found

the courage to go and talk to a doctor about my eating disorder. Although seeking medical help was something I had thought of many times throughout my struggle with bulimia, I had never been able to bring myself to do it. I told myself I was fine and that I didn't need that much help. But as I began unravelling some of the deep-seated fears and beliefs I had around asking for help, I began to feel less and less resistance to talking with a professional.

Early one morning a few weeks back I had found the courage to do so. I had gone to the doctor Sarah recommended and, just like all of the other times I had been afraid to have a conversation, this encounter was no different: it went well. It was my internal critic that had overreacted, previously stopping me from seeking help. The doctor had not judged me or told me I was stupid and weak. He had reassured me I had not done any irreversible damage to my body through bingeing and purging, and he gave me a number of resources to help me continue to improve my health. What I was most grateful for was, he had cared. I had left with renewed hope and a positive outlook.

"Well, that was a successful afternoon," I laughed as I unlocked my front door, feeling another layer of the stubborn independence that had been my armour for years fall away.

"I guess asking for help isn't so bad after all."

Chapter 5—First Taste of Entrepreneurship

Serious Inspiration

"Happy lawyers in Toronto?" My mind reeled. I had just enjoyed an hour-long conference call with Rubsun Ho, one of the founding partners of Cognition LLP, and Lesley Croll Henry, Cognition's Director of Lawyer and Client Happiness. I could barely believe that this kind of law firm existed. I put down the phone and stared at the five pages of scrawl I had furiously generated as they told me about their alternative open-office-concept law firm, which, at the time, had enticed thirty-one stressed-out Toronto lawyers off the beaten path from traditional "Big Law." Not only that, the firm had marketing professionals to handle the business side of the practice, a Charter of Values, and a Director of Lawyer and Client Happiness. I was smiling from ear to ear as I sat down to write my latest installment of my lawyers-loving-life series on TYS.

Over the past month I had become increasingly interested in researching alternative legal practices and innovation in the legal profession. On June 12, 2013, I set myself a challenge to write one inspiring blog post per day for a week about lawyers loving life. The first article I wrote had been about my discovery of Axiom, which was at the time a thousand-person law firm operating in eleven offices and four delivery centres across three continents. Stumbling across Axiom on my Twitter feed (which I had started using to follow hundreds of legal experts, innovators, and law firms across the globe) opened my eyes to alternative legal practice in practice! It was my first glimpse at a big law firm reinventing how to provide legal services and also acknowledging that lawyers are passionate people with interests both inside and outside the law.

I spent all my spare time in the next six days scouring Twitter, and searching the web for other inspiring stories to tell, successfully producing articles on the deregulation of legal services, virtual law firms, an initiative by Axiom called RethinkLaw, new articling initiatives, flexible work arrangements, and finally ending with a post I called "Axiom in Vancouver?!" in which I recounted my interview of a local law firm doing things differently.

Researching and writing seven articles in seven days had been a challenge I thoroughly enjoyed. Although I did not continue with the same volume as that first week, my interest in writing inspiring stories about lawyers doing things differently persisted. I wrote articles about two thought leaders in legal innovation, Mitch Kowalski and Jordan Furlong; a two-part interview series with a local young lawyer who had overcome a number of challenges, eventually starting up his own law practice; and today, I found myself excitedly writing about a group of happy lawyers in Toronto. Smiling, I pushed "publish" on my latest post. I was starting to get a sense that I wasn't alone in my desire for passion and innovation in the legal profession.

Courageous Action

"Uh ... I felt like I didn't have any ownership over my career, and also I felt kind of isolated, like I couldn't talk about these things ... because as a lawyer you just suck it up and power through, or you leave the profession. So, I started this blog to write about those issues and to hopefully find another way ... and ... um ... so, I'm sure some of you have felt some of

Chapter 5

those frustrations at some points in time, and I just want to say that, that's not what this event is all about. We're not going to be talking about the problems. We're not going to be talking about frustrations or stresses. What I would like to talk about instead is … the ideal, so … what we would like to have in the alternative …. What would you love to have as a career? What would be the ideal in this profession for you?"

My voice carried out into the room of young lawyers, pausing with nervous "Um"s and "So"s, as I went on to explain the speed networking activity we would be engaging in to discuss our career ideals. It was the evening of July 25, 2013, and my first TYS event—Young Lawyers Loving Life—was in full swing. A lot had gone in to putting the event together, from creating flyers and advertising through social media and asking friends and young lawyers interested in the TYS mission to spread the event through word of mouth, to obtaining a liquor licence, booking a venue, preparing materials, buying food, setting up the room, and asking a good friend who was a photographer to take a few pictures and a short video for the blog recap.

And now it was happening! The tables were filled with question prompts, agendas, colourful recipe cards, pens, plates, napkins, partially consumed snacks and drinks. The faces of about twenty young lawyers stared up at me. I was incredibly nervous standing in front of other young lawyers to share the TYS mission with the intention of creating an environment where we would all feel comfortable to talk about some of our dreams and our fears. I was realizing it was one thing to blog about my experience and the changes I was making, but to actually share in front of a group who might at any moment judge me, laugh at me or, worse yet, sit silently smiling and then whisper to each other later about how ridiculous I was engaged a completely different level of fear. I looked down at my page of notes, shakily held in my right hand, not really seeing them, and continued on.

After completing my introductory speech, the speed networking began, with young lawyers pairing off to discuss their ideal work schedule, place of work, type of work, career mentorship, work environment, and level of control and responsibility. As a swell of conversation rose up around me, I took a sip of water for my dry throat and a couple of deep breaths, trying to release the tension in my shoulders.

I focused on gathering up courage for the remainder of the evening.

This wasn't the only event that I had taken on as part of the plan I had generated with my life coach to turn my passions into a business helping young lawyers to trash their stress and create lives they love. I thought back to a few weeks earlier when I had taken on another terrifying action in service of growing my business: cold calling. I remembered the agonizing hours of staring at my neatly compiled spreadsheet of names and numbers, using every means of motivation I could think of—from pleading to enticing to threatening—to convince myself to pick up the phone and dial the first number. My stomach had lurched so ferociously the first time that I hung up before anyone had answered. I remembered the first few bumbling conversations with career services and human resources staff at law schools and law firms, trying to stick to my carefully crafted script, while the person on the other end asked me questions that made it impossible.

I reminded myself how, around conversation number ten, after hearing many versions of—"You are calling about what? Sorry, not interested."—even the rejection had become easier. By conversation twenty I had begun speaking passionately and laughing with the often-incredulous person on the other end, without a glance toward the scripted conversation beside me. I smiled as I remembered the first conversation, about thirty calls in, that had generated positive interest, and a few more conversations later hearing a *yes*, to my proposal to put on a workshop on stress and ideal career arrangements for young lawyers. I was now in conversation with a lovely woman at career services at the University of Ottawa Faculty of Law, discussing details of what would be TYS's first lunchtime workshop for law students, including timing and compensation.

I had found the courage to overcome so many of my fears to get to where I was standing today—hosting my first evening event for young lawyers in Vancouver.

"You're simply having a conversation with other young lawyers. You've done this hundreds of times," I reassured myself as the timer went off ending the last round of speed networking and I turned back toward my audience.

The next few hours at Young Lawyers Loving Life flew by as the speed networking transitioned into an open discussion about the barriers in the way of our career ideals and then into brainstorming ways we might overcome the barriers. Interspersed between the discussions were breaks when everyone had the opportunity to mingle and connect over snacks and drinks. By the end of the evening I was glowing, no longer from nerves but from the connections and inspiration shared. A different conversation had been had among young lawyers: one of possibility, instead of frustration.

Merciless Scrutiny and Reluctant Forgiveness

As incredible as Young Lawyers Loving Life had been and as much as I tried to stay positive in the days that followed, my mind began dissecting the event and measuring it against my own impossible expectations. I had ordered too much food. I had not attracted the numbers I had anticipated. I had not executed my speech in the perfect manner I intended. Also, it had been a lot of work, and, over all, I had lost money. My carefully crafted business plan milestone had not been met in the way I had imagined. I began to label the event and myself as failures.

Half of me felt awful because the event (and the rest of my projects) hadn't turned out perfectly so far, and half of me didn't care and just wanted to throw everything away. I began rethinking my plan to make a business out of my passions. Actually, I began rethinking everything. As soon as I started labelling one thing as a failure, everything else in my internal world began to take a downward turn: I didn't like the way my body looked or felt; I was sad I wasn't in a romantic relationship; I was angry at myself for not being productive enough at my part-time law work; I was frustrated that I was not motivated; I was indecisive about the direction to take my blog and my business. The list continued.

I was also sad because I knew my relationship with Sarah was coming to an end. I had signed up for three months of coaching at the beginning of May. At the end of July I hadn't been ready to let go. I had decided to hire Sarah for one more month. But now, having lost money on my event, and having put most of my time toward my business in July and, therefore, not making very much money practising as a lawyer, I simply could not justify continuing with life coaching. The practical advice my parents had ground into me since I was a child was in the forefront of my awareness: never spend more than you make. As much as I was still getting a lot of value from our sessions, I couldn't justify the continued expense. I decided that August would be my last month. And so I was sad on top of

Chapter 5

feeling like a failure. I began reverting with more frequency to my coping mechanism of busyness and food to numb the pain. I was frustrated with my relapse.

Sarah was helpful through all of this. She reflected that my relationship to results was either attached or resigned (neither of which, I admitted, was really working for me). She asked what relationship I would like it to be instead. I thought, wouldn't it be nice if I didn't attach my personal worth to what I was doing *and* didn't give up on creating a life I loved. And wouldn't it be nice if I stopped being so indecisive about what I wanted and just went for it and kept at it.

Sarah suggested it sounded like what I was looking for was clarity and commitment. I agreed.

So it was back to the drawing board. But first I had to clear it of the mess my internal critic had made in my head, which meant it was time for more completion: feeling the emotions; taking responsibility; and coming to acceptance, forgiveness, and letting go. What was really going on was I was scared to put myself out there and host another event for young lawyers, and also scared of how I might screw up the two lunchtime workshops I was now scheduled to put on for law students in October; my critic was trying to convince me not to do those.

The completion exercise that Sarah recommended I take on around how my business had gone so far helped. I was beginning to let go of all the negative feelings about my first event and everything else I had been labelling a failure. I did some visioning and got reconnected to the projects I had been working on. As had become my new normal, I shared the entire process on my blog as I went.

Find a Way to Begin Again

It was Sunday, August 25, 2013, and I was sitting in Calhoun's twenty-four-hour coffee shop trying to write my maid-of-honour speech for the wedding of one of my best friends the following weekend. I was stumped, just like I had been stumped at coming up with an idea of what to write for my second blog post that week. I had been listening to maid-of-honour speeches on YouTube for the past half hour, hoping to get inspired. In this latest one, the woman had bought a lottery ticket, choosing numbers which for some reason related to the bride, and then given her speech using those numbers before handing the lottery ticket over to the couple. It was so cheesy. It was perfect!

Half an hour later, after much reminiscing, I had chosen my numbers and was nearly done writing my speech for my friend's wedding next weekend. The words were flowing out of me. How could I have forgotten that my life was filled with so much love and that writing was such fun? I wanted more. I laughed to myself as I pulled up a new Word document and began typing:

This week I've been struggling with what to write about. I looked at my to-do list on Thursday and it said, "Write inspiring blog post." It could be the perfect interview, the most inspiring story, or basically anything that would blow people away.

"Easy task," I had thought sarcastically. "It only had to be amazing. No pressure." I was frustrated because I didn't have it. I hadn't done the perfect interview; I hadn't researched an inspiring story; and I didn't feel like I had material that would blow anyone away. I chastised myself for not having reached out to someone to interview, for not having scoured Twitter for the latest legal innovation news to

Chapter 5

share and, even as my mind asked, "Well, why don't you do that then?" I still did not do it. I wasn't motivated.

Thursday came and went, and so did Friday, and then it was Saturday and I still didn't have a good story. I started and restarted a couple of posts but didn't like them. So I scrapped them. I thought, maybe I won't write a second post this week. I made excuses: I'd been busier at work; I'd been running more; I'd been helping some of my closest friends get ready for their wedding next weekend; I'd just been too busy.

And then tonight as I was writing my maid-of-honour speech, I suddenly felt the urge to write more. I felt the urge to share. Actually I just felt a lot. I felt excited. I felt grateful. I felt happy. I felt love. So I'm writing.

I realised that I had made writing into a chore. Writing this blog is something I love. But I wasn't approaching it from a place of love. I was approaching it from a place of "have to." I was approaching it as a means to an end, rather than an end in and of itself. And it was stifling my ability to write at all.

So tonight I'm writing from love. And I'm writing about the importance of being in whatever you are doing. You can call it awareness. You can call it presence. You can call it living in the moment. For me, it means coming from love. It means actually feeling and bringing love into what I am doing as I am doing it. It means offering a piece of myself in my work and being grateful for the opportunity to share. And it's such an amazing place to be.

I paused and smiled as I thought back on the past weeks and months. Sometime the previous week I had released myself from my internal critic's clutches long enough to have some fun at work with my colleagues. I remembered a long conversation in Jamie's office involving a string of funny stories and banter, ending with a request that I write up a memo on one of the other partner's poor clothing style so we could stage an intervention. That day I wrote a blog post about the importance of laughter. For the first time since my demon had labelled my event a failure and taken me down with it, I had brought in some levity, and was starting to see the positives.

Basking in the positive head space I now had, I thought back even further to the gratitude challenge I had completed as part of Scott Dinsmore's "How to Connect with Anyone" course earlier in the spring. I smiled at the thought of the little love notes I had left in hiding places all over the city, and the letters I'd sent out to some close friends and friends I had lost touch with, thanking them for being who they are and for who they have been for me.

Grateful that my inner demon was taking a much-needed nap, I scrolled through my photos on my computer remembering even more silly times and fun adventures with friends, including the other two weddings of close friends I had been a part of earlier in the year. I turned back to my writing, infusing my post with even more gratitude and love, before signing off with my usual "xo, Danielle" and looking around the Sunday night café filled with students and doodlers and writers like me. I felt connected to everyone.

"This is it," I thought. "Being in the doing."

The storm of the previous month had subsided. I had completely let go of the judgments I had been holding on myself around how my business had gone so far, and although I would miss talking with Sarah every week I felt strong in all I had learned. I was ready to let her go. I could feel a familiar buzz of excitement in my gut as I thought of the upcoming workshops I had scheduled for the fall. I was back! And I was *so* grateful.

Chapter 6—Tending to the Fire

Seizing Every Spark

What you do really does matter. Of course it does.

All it takes is a moment of inspiration. An idea. One stroke of passion, a burst of confidence, of hope. The belief that you really can make a difference. That your actions really do matter. You matter.

What you do really does matter.

Of course it does.

We don't often realize the power of an idea, a word, a laugh, a smile, a feeling.

These moments are all around us; if only we allowed ourselves to be moved by them. To be open. To be vulnerable. To feel a little more passionately.

Allow yourself to believe in what you believe in. Allow yourself to hope for what you hope for.

If you love something, truly love it. If you love someone, truly love that person. That's where true courage lies. That's where true power lies.

Allow yourself to feel. Allow yourself to believe. Allow yourself to lean into the amazingness of being human, because that's the only way anything meaningful happens.

That's the only way meaningful work happens. The only way meaningful connection happens. The only way meaningful change happens.

It's the only way you will contribute to this world all that you have to offer. And it's the only way you will love each moment of each day that you are given.

I Am Enough

Each of us can make a difference. And together we can create the changes we only catch a glimpse of in our wildest dreams.

All it takes is a moment of inspiration.

My fingers tapped passionately on my iPhone screen as I wandered slowly down the streets of downtown Vancouver and over the Burrard Street Bridge, pausing between bursts of writing to stare at the stars and the moon and the gleam of city lights sparkling on the ocean.

This kind of inspired writing was becoming increasingly common for me since I had watched a TED talk by spoken word poet Sarah Kay called "If I should have a daughter ..." a few months earlier. The talk had reminded me how much I love poetry and had inspired me to try something different; not formal poetry, but something more poetic than my usual blog posts. I felt peace flowing through me as I let words flow from somewhere deeper, some place bigger than me. No purpose. No predetermined message or theme. I was alive to a creative part in me I'd long forgotten.

It was mid-November and I was walking home from a Liberal Party of Canada fundraiser and celebration of Hedy Fry's twentieth anniversary of her election as MP for Vancouver Centre. I had never been to a Liberal Party event before and hadn't really known what to expect. Before arriving I had tried to clear my mind of all judgments and expectations (like it would be stuffy and boring, and I wouldn't know anyone). I must have succeeded because this is what happened: I was inspired. I was inspired by Hedy Fry's passion and her love of life that shone through and across the room. I was blown away by the dedication she had inspired in the few hundred people who had gathered in her honour, and no doubt in thousands more who could only attend in spirit.

Chapter 6

My heart was filled with gratitude for the evening, and for the man who had invited me, Dave. Although our rekindled relationship was only a few weeks in, I was excited. This time felt different.

When Dave and I had first begun dating halfway into my clerkship year in early 2011, I had not been ready for a serious relationship. I had known I would be leaving six months later to article in Manitoba. What I had been looking for at the time was some shared passion and a little fun. After a month or so, it had become clear that we were on different pages and we had parted ways.

When I returned to Vancouver after my articles, Dave and I had reconnected, and our friendship had quickly turned into something more romantic. But again, the voices tormenting me from the inside had not let me be happy with what we had. I had grown restless, told myself that despite the fact that he was exactly the kind of guy I was looking for, we just didn't have the right chemistry; he wasn't the one. I had ended our budding relationship again after a few months.

Now, nearly a year of internal examination and transformation later, I knew my restless dissatisfaction had been driven by my own internal demon. A couple of weeks back, I had gathered up my courage and reached out, shared honestly that I missed having him in my life, and asked if he would be willing to try again. He had been. I was looking forward to a new journey with him as part of creating this life I loved, and grateful that he'd been willing to give us another chance. I smiled at the memories flooding my blissed-out mind, letting them wander from my romantic relationship to my recent business successes and the amazing people who had made their way into my life.

The first memory that came to mind was of an interview I'd done a couple of months back with Michael McCubbin, a young lawyer who had started his own firm straight out of articling. Mike, who at the time of the interview had been running a successful law firm for nearly two years, spent a good hour telling me how he had got started. It was a whirlwind of a tale, something you might make a movie about, and from start to finish I had been enthralled.

I had been so inspired by Mike I had shared the full interview on my blog, and had asked him to be a guest speaker at my upcoming event for young lawyers. The event was on ideal work arrangements, and I had thought who better to speak than someone who had had a dream and had gone out there and created it. The second speaker at the event had been my former life coach, Sarah. Between Sarah's positive energy and Mike's practical advice, we had all been left inspired and with proof that if you know what you want and go for it, anything is possible.

Flying on the inspiration from my second successful event, I had landed halfway across the country in early October ready to inspire some law students to trash their stress and create a life they loved. As I had curled up on the couch of a good friend in Toronto the night before my first lunchtime workshop, I had been nervous, but mostly I had just felt full. I had been overcome with love for the life I was creating and for all of the people who were helping me to create it. I had felt my heart would surely burst with the gratitude that had been welling up. I knew that if it had not been for the supportive environment at my law firm, my family, my friends, my former coach, and the growing community of young lawyers getting behind what I was up to, I likely would not have had the courage to call up the law schools in the first place and offer my services, nor to make a trip half way across the country to put on workshops in my first year of business.

Chapter 6

As I had sat in the cafeteria at Osgoode Hall Law School the next morning preparing some notes and enjoying the excited buzz of students milling around me, I had been transported back in time. The students had been rehashing their weekends, making case-law jokes that only those who have been to law school could ever find funny, and frantically asking each other about the readings they had not yet done. Having done all of the above a few years earlier, I had sat there feeling nostalgic, and also a little less nervous about the workshop I was about to put on.

Although I had arrived feeling nervous, the only way to describe the way I had felt hours later when I left Osgoode Hall was inspired. And as I sat down to write my blog recap a few days later after another amazing lunchtime workshop with the law students at the University of Ottawa, I had been again, blissfully inspired.

I pulled up the blog post I had written on my iPhone as I continued my blissful walk home, and scrolled down, stopping to re-read the last paragraphs.

And what I am most grateful for, after spending some time with the students this week, is not only did it bring back memories of some great times in my life, but it gave me a glimpse of the infinite possibility that exists for the future of our profession.

Can you imagine what the legal profession would look like in ten years if each student who graduated knew their dreams and was prepared to take their career into their own hands to make those dreams happen? Can you imagine if each graduate believed without question that it were possible to create a life that they love in this profession? Can you imagine if each student had the tools and resources needed to put a plan in place to achieve their ideal career, and the support network necessary to carry them through challenges, overcome barriers, and actually make it happen? Can you imagine the creative alternative law practices that would be dreamed up and built, each tailored to a lawyer's strengths, and each allowing the lawyer to most effectively offer his or her unique services to the world?

I imagine these things all the time, because it is my dream for our profession. And I am so grateful for the students this week for giving me a glimpse of that dream in action.

"Yes," I thought, "the past couple of months have been filled with inspiration and connection." I put my phone back in my pocket as I arrived at my front door, the beginning of a blog post on the topic of inspiration forming in my head.

Walking the Blazing Trail

"Maybe I should take the paragraph about the meetings out," I thought. "Is it really important? Probably not. Plus, if we say that, we'd have to attach the spreadsheet the paragraph refers to. Would that be a good idea? I don't know. I'd need to run that by Jamie."

I touched my phone on the table beside me: 2:35 a.m. it said. I was staying over at Dave's and I could not sleep. I was restless; enthusiastically drafting legal affidavits in my head in the middle of the night. I turned over and sighed at the sight of Dave peacefully asleep beside me.

"That should be me right now," I thought, trying once again to quiet the incessant stream of ideas running through my mind. I curled up on my side, tucked the blankets up under my chin, and closed my eyes. My efforts went unnoticed by my restless mind.

"Actually, if I organized the whole affidavit in time periods,

Chapter 6

that would make more sense. Of course! That's a great idea." I was physically itching with adrenaline and anticipation. There was no fighting the creation going on in my head. As quietly as I could, I got up, dressed, and slipped out into the night.

Fifteen minutes later, after a quick stop at the twenty-four-hour coffee shop a few blocks from Dave's apartment, I was nearly at my law office. I looked up from my buzzing ideas, as a man in tattered clothing pulling a suitcase encased in mud passed by on my left muttering to himself. My mind flashed back to my middle-of-the-night articling commutes and the reality of what I was doing hit me.

I stopped short.

"Maybe, I am wrong," I thought. "Maybe it really isn't possible to achieve 'balance' in this profession. Maybe if I want to be a great lawyer, I have to accept the fact that I'm going to be a little crazy; that work might get out of control sometimes, and I might lose sleep and other things that are important to me, including myself."

My energy drained to the ground. It was the week before Christmas and I'd been really busy at work for nearly two months. A few weeks earlier I had written a blog post offering ten ways to maintain sanity in times of busyness. While I had been practising most of the things I had written about, rule ten—make sure you have an end date for the period of busyness—kept getting pushed back. I knew at some point there would have to be an end, but November had closed, and I had taken on December at the same pace. I had been flying around on high speed balancing long hours at work with weekly blog posts, Christmas parties, lunch dates with friends, hanging out with Dave, and a year-end meetup for TYS. Now, staring at the glass doors of my office building at 3:00 a.m. on a Tuesday, all I could think was: "Am I a hypocrite? How could

I be writing about maintaining sanity if I can't even play by my own rules?"

But then I noticed something else, or rather the absence of something that was usually present in times of working in the middle of the night: stress. My stony stance relaxed. I could feel the excitement that had been coursing through me moments earlier building and itching to return.

"My work wasn't 'out of control.' I hadn't lost anything. Maybe things were a little crazy, but I was enjoying it. I felt alive. I was happy."

Excitement came back in waves.

"I love getting absorbed in things completely," I thought. "I choose to let myself get wrapped up in them. I do this in all areas of my life. I choose to allow myself to care deeply because that's when I do my best work. That's when I make my greatest contribution to whatever I am doing, and to others."

I reached for my office keys and buzzed myself into the building and up the elevator to the twentieth floor. I thought of my life the same time the previous year. I had been very busy at work, but the feeling was different. While I had been mostly enjoying what I was doing, work felt separate from life. It had felt like something I *had* to do, something that was taking me away from time I could spend living.

"Now work feels like time I am spending living," I thought. "I will not always choose to make work the part of my life that takes up most of my time, but in the past couple of months I have. And what makes it okay is just that. I choose it. I now know my priorities. I know what is important to me."

As I sat down at my desk and powered on my computer I started giggling. I could have chosen to care less; I could have chosen to sleep; but at that moment I was choosing to draft affidavits. For some reason this was hilarious to me. That I could be happy at 3:00 a.m. drafting affidavits was a little hard to admit, but the truth is that it did make me happy.

"Alright then, let's do this," I thought. I took a sip of coffee, leaned forward, and dove in.

Cleaning out the Hearth

Two weeks later, fully rested, I was curled up with a cup of coffee on my parents' couch in Manitoba in front of the Christmas tree. I was about to dive in to another kind of work. Through my nerves I could feel a familiar mix of fear and excitement. I turned back to my journal flipped open on my lap in front of me and wrote, "Failures."

I didn't really want to do it. I knew it would be the hardest part of my year-end reflection, or at least the most painful. I was mostly looking forward to the second part of this exercise—achievements—but I knew this first part was necessary.

"You want a balanced picture, Danielle," I reminded myself, "and a clean slate to dream up your goals for next year. Just start."

In 2013, I had given myself permission to dream. For the first time my creative ideas were no longer limited to the legal problem I was working on or where I would travel to next: my entire life was on the table to be imagined and rewritten. I had surprised myself with the level of inspiration and imagination I had access to quite naturally. It had been a lot easier than I thought to discover things I was passionate about and to create a beautiful vision for how I would bring those things into my life. I was also starting to realize I was something of an inspiration junkie. I loved falling in love with new ideas, people, places, or things, and getting really excited about them, whether or not I brought them into the world to completion.

While many of my sparks had created lasting fires, many had flickered and faded. I took a deep breath and put my pen to the page:

1. **Get funding to support Trash Your Stress projects.** Sent letters to Law Societies and other organizations, attaching a detailed funding proposal. No response. Didn't follow up.
2. **Create an online course for young lawyers.** Started making the course in May, worked on it here and there for the next few months. Did not finish.
3. **Offer stress coaching services to lawyers.** Started exchanging stress coaching for motivational speaking coaching with a speech therapist in October. Went to networking events and talked about it. No lawyers became clients in 2013.
4. **Start a local mastermind group.** Talked to a few people but did not make it happen.
5. **Remake Al Pacino's "Inches" speech from *Any Given Sunday* into an inspirational speech for lawyers.** Did it. Did not share it with anyone except my little brother.
6. **Do a TED Talk.** Talked with Sarah about it. Did not take any action (other than beginning motivational speaking coaching).
7. **Speak at law firms regarding stress.** Did some cold calls. No law firms interested.
8. **Speak at high schools about stress.** Hired a virtual assistant from the Philippines to compile a spreadsheet of contact information for all the high schools in BC. Did not call any.
9. **Make a Trash Your Stress presentation at a legal conference.** Was asked to do this. Prepared material for the conference. Conference was cancelled.
10. **Create a free eBook that people receive when they sign up for my blog newsletter.** Created a few shorter free resources. The eBook never happened.

Chapter 6

As I came to an end of my list I felt better than I thought I would, lighter, grateful even. "I have learned a lot this year," I thought. And then I turned to a blank page and began listing all of the things I had achieved and the fires that were still burning. There were many.

I thought back even further.

At the end of 2012, I had been working fifty-plus hours a week, bingeing and purging on average three times a week, and getting four to five hours of sleep a night. One year after that fateful moment when I cancelled my 5:30 a.m. run, although I was still bingeing, I had stopped purging my food completely, and was reinventing my relationship to food and my body. I had let go of a lot of the comparing of myself to other women, and in particular, my sister; we were closer than ever before. I was working fifteen to thirty hours a week at my law firm and I was sleeping an average of six hours a night. My business, although not yet profitable, was starting to take off. In 2013, I had started a blog; written over one hundred blog posts; connected with entrepreneurs all over the world through Live Your Legend; learned how to use social media; posted an inspirational quote, video, or post online nearly every day; shared a weekly newsletter with my TYS readers; held three events for young lawyers in Vancouver; flown out to Ottawa and Toronto to put on workshops at law schools; learned about alternative legal processes; hired a life coach; interviewed inspiring people in the legal community; and helped many young lawyers deal with stress.

Although I had not achieved all the goals I had set out to, I felt a sense of peace and confidence in the changes I had made so far. I knew the biggest changes I was making were on the inside. Not only was the tiny shift that had begun within me at 11:00 p.m. on January 6, 2013 still alive and strong: it was spreading like wildfire. I thought back to a few weeks earlier when I'd started this reflection process, and the blog post I'd written that had pulled the internal changes together: "The Five Greatest Lessons Learned in 2013." To remind myself of what I had learned I flipped open my lap top and re-read the five lessons I had shared.

1. I am enough

This past year I have become more aware of the expectations I place on myself to be something other than, or "more" than, who I am.

I used to consistently define myself by doing; by achieving things, and crossing items off to-do lists. I would place so many expectations of perfection on myself that no matter how hard I tried, I would never get there. It was never enough. I was never enough.

I admit I still struggle with this—but more and more I am operating from a place of "enough." I am learning that enough is the place from which all life grows. It is the place from which all great achievements start and all great contributions are made. It is also a pretty amazing place to be.

2. Gratitude

Incorporating more expressions of gratitude into my life has been one of the most lifesaving habits I have created this year. I am much more aware on a daily basis of the many things I have to be grateful for than I was at the beginning of the year, and I have seen the profound effect this awareness has had on my overall wellbeing.

Taking a moment at the end of the day to write out a few things that I am grateful for allows me to step back from the busyness of my day and gain perspective on what's important in my life and to go to bed with my mind at peace with what is.

Chapter 6

Reflecting on those little moments from the day also enables me to learn what truly makes me happy so that I can incorporate more of those moments into my life.

3. Connection

At the beginning of this year, connection was something I thought I was pretty good at. But as I began experimenting in search of what was missing in my life, I realised that, to a large extent, it was connection. Real connection.

I realised that although I had all kinds of relationships in my life, I was often relating on a superficial level. I rarely allowed the relationship to scratch below the surface. I couldn't bear to let others see the entire me. It was too real. But that's just it. It has to scratch below the surface to mean anything. That's when connection counts. That's when life moves to a new level.

Connection at a deeper level has been one of the most (if not the most) important changes I have made this year. It has reduced my stress levels; helped me to stop catastrophizing; increased my confidence, happiness, and my overall well-being; opened up new opportunities; and has allowed me to experience moments where nothing is "missing" from my life.

4. The Common Element: LOVE

These three lessons above have a common element. They have a shared current that gives them power. And that is love.

I bring love into my life a million times more now than I ever have before. I bring love to each of my relationships, and I try to bring love into each of my actions. I even bring love into my work, which previously I believed was impossible.

5. The Common Cause: Vulnerability

All of the lessons above have a common cause, a common enabler. And that is vulnerability.

This year I realized that there was a huge part of myself that I had been hiding. I had surrounded myself with so many walls because I was terrified to be open. I refused to allow myself to be vulnerable with anyone. As I gained courage to allow myself to be seen, I gained an increased capacity for love in all areas of my life and an appreciation of the power of vulnerability. I've come to believe that all of the changes I have made this year are as a result of just that: the courage to be vulnerable; to allow myself to be seen.

I stopped reading and looked up. There were tears of joy in my eyes. "Things really are different in my internal world," I thought. "Overall, I haven't been this happy and peaceful since I was a child."

Throw on Some More Wood

"What does your heart say?" The deep powerful voice of the man on the other end of the phone line caught me off guard.

"Do lawyers really ask you to listen to your heart? This isn't how I thought this would go," I thought, even though I had no business predicting how this conversation would go. I had constantly been surprised by Sarah Kalil, the first lawyer-turned-life-coach I had met. I don't know why I thought this second one would be predictable.

Adam Quiney was patiently waiting for me to speak and the silence was killing me. Adam was one of the leaders at Accomplishment Coaching (AC), a twelve-month life coach and leadership training program in Seattle. I had expressed

Chapter 6

interest in taking the course and he was following up to see if I had made a decision to enroll starting in January 2014. I knew the answer to his question, but I didn't want to answer, so I stalled.

"Well, you know, it sounds great but I'm just not sure I can afford it," I said. "And I've got a lot going on already. I don't want to take on too much."

Adam listened to my well-thought-out diversions patiently, with loads of understanding and a bit of playful banter, before coming back around to the question I still hadn't answered.

"And what does your heart say?"

"That's just the trouble," I thought, half wishing he would have forgotten the question, half grateful he hadn't, "my heart is screaming 'Yes.' But my mind … my mind is full of reasons why I should not."

I knew that my excuses of not having enough time or money were just that, excuses. I had enough money saved up to pay for the year-long transformational leadership and life-coaching program up front, and my schedule was now mine to fill, so how could I not have time unless I said I didn't have time?

I thought back to the dimly lit tavern I had found myself in a few weeks earlier. I had been sitting across from Sarah, sipping a beer at a slightly worn wooden high-top table along the wall across from the bar. I felt warmth at the memory. I had spent most of the evening on the edge of my seat, head propped on my hand, transfixed by the life-filled words flowing from the woman across from me. Although our coaching relationship had completed a few months earlier, Sarah and I had remained friends. She had been telling me about her experience as a participant in the AC program this past year. She had just graduated a few weeks earlier. She told me her graduation had been one of the best days of her life.

I Am Enough

"It was like a wedding with myself," she had said.

When I had met Sarah in February before ever engaging her for life coaching, I hadn't thought it possible that the positive energy she exuded could expand any more, but the woman sitting in front of me in December had changed. I could feel love pouring out toward me in every word she spoke. It was like she carried around a force field of joy and love, and if you got close enough you would be sucked in and get high on life. I was leaning in. I wanted what she had.

Ever since that conversation, my heart had been screaming yes to enrolling in the AC program and embarking on a year of deep transformation of my own, and although my mind had quickly constructed a number of walls to protect me, I could still feel it.

"My heart says yes," I heard myself reply almost inaudibly.

And then, as if the spell of silence I had put my heart under had been broken, I spoke again, more boldly.

"Yes! My heart says yes."

I was in.

That mid-December telephone conversation had set the tone for my year-end visioning; I was ready to dream bigger. As I sat down a few weeks later on December 30, 2013 to reflect on my goals for the New Year, I was excited. It felt like anything was possible. My heart spoke boldly as I began to write my goals on the page.

1. **Law**: More court experience, more responsibility, more pro bono
2. **Travel**: World Domination Summit weekend in Portland; three weeks in Brazil and Peru
3. **TYS**: Write and publish a book on Creating a Life You LOVE in Law

4. **Blog**: Write fifty blog posts and five articles for other publications
5. **Personal**: Complete and graduate from twelve-month Accomplishment Coaching Program
6. **Health**: Continue to develop positive habits, more sleep, less emotional eating
7. **Fitness**: Run a marathon
8. **Relationships**: More communication, more gratitude, more vulnerability
9. **Financial**: Increase my earnings by 25% and save all of it
10. **Giving Back**: Volunteer three hours a month with an eating disorder program in Vancouver

When I finished, I read over the list, and my stomach began to churn. I closed the book, terrified. These goals were huge, and I could hear a familiar voice telling me they were impossible. But my heart was stronger. I took a deep breath, reopened my journal and continued.

My intention for 2014 is to let my light shine even more. To set aside my fears and courageously step into my own greatness. To dream big. To love completely. To live fully.

My motto for 2014 is "Nothing is Impossible."

Each day I will repeat this with conviction. Each day I will find courage in my heart and recommit to myself. And that is what will make 2014 my best year yet!

Chapter 7—The War on Goals

The Battle Begins

A few days into 2014, it began. Reality set in: I had set some really big goals. It was 9:00 a.m. on Saturday of the first weekend in January, and I had arrived at the fortieth floor of the Columbia Tower in downtown Seattle for the first weekend of my AC program. I was greeted by about a dozen different AC leaders and ushered into a large conference room where my twenty-three new teammates were nervously milling around, sipping coffee and eyeing each other up.

"What have I gotten myself into?" I thought. After a long week since writing out my goals and a spotty night of sleep, my belief in my ability to complete the course on top of everything else I wanted to do was wavering.

As we dove into the day my teammates and I were each invited to the front of the room to share who we were, why we were there, and what our goals were for the year. We were then offered powerful reflections of our greatness and our blocks on the spot by the leaders as we stood in front of everyone. It was a vulnerable experience. By the end of the day I was completely exhausted, both mentally and physically from my lack of sleep and my long week, and emotionally from baring my heart in front of a room full of strangers.

"This is only day one of weekend one of twelve weekends," my head warned me later that evening as I curled up in my little hotel room after dinner and a beer with Daniel and Steve, two of my new teammates who were also from Vancouver. "You have committed to coming down to Seattle for this kind of uncomfortable experience the first weekend of every month for the entire year. I doubt the next eleven weekends will be any less challenging. Plus, there is the course material itself that you need to learn. You will never be able to complete this!"

I contemplated jumping in the car I had rented for the weekend, driving back to Vancouver and not even showing up for day two. But then I remembered my motto for the year—Nothing is Impossible. I decided to get some sleep and at least stick it out for one more day. By the end of Sunday, I had made some new friends and been paired with my coach, Rachelle (Bay) LeBlanc Quiney—one of the leaders helping to put on the AC program and the other half of the team of Quiney coaches. I rallied my confidence and decided to stay.

"You can do this." I told myself as I curled up in my own bed back in Vancouver late Sunday evening. "This is exactly the kind of challenge you wanted for yourself this year. One that is uncomfortable. One that will require you to transform and grow."

A few days later, overwhelm made its second attack. I was having my first coaching session with Bay and we were discussing the goals I had set for myself for the year. I was trying to be excited but feelings of overwhelm were growing. I could see the next two weeks on my calendar full of things—all things I had chosen and all things I loved to do—but right then all I could see was the huge number of them.

Nagging voices began swirling in my head. "You didn't get as much done today as you wanted. You didn't get as much done yesterday as you wanted. How do you expect to catch up on those things and do everything you want to do tomorrow, and the next day, and the next day, and the next day? You are clearly going to fail! You might as well set smaller goals for yourself now, so I don't have to say 'I told you so' later."

Chapter 7

Bay and I took a look at the pattern I was continually replaying, which went something like this: get really excited about a bunch of new goals; set impossible expectations; start taking action really excitedly; fail to meet one of my impossible expectations; pretend it's fine and try harder; cut out sleep and self-care; feel more and more exhausted and overwhelmed; withdraw, crash, and feel like a failure; get some kind of support and inspiration; and then repeat the whole thing again.

We discussed how I might, when I was hit with the feelings of overwhelm, choose something other than the withdrawal and disappointment that was predictable for me. By the end of the call I felt better. I had a plan: I would try reaching out to someone when I was feeling overwhelmed instead of hiding.

That night I went with my boyfriend Dave to his friend's place to play Trivia, and again overwhelm had been on the attack: all I could think about were the things I wasn't getting done. I was totally wrapped up in my head. I could feel myself withdrawing from conversation. I was aware of what I was doing, but couldn't seem to stop it. It was like I was sitting in a cloud floating high above my head watching myself run out into a busy street. There was nothing I could do about it. I was heading straight for disappointment.

Back at Dave's place at the end of the evening, I was about to withdraw completely when my awareness trickled down to the part of me that remained engaged in my life on the ground. I remembered I could choose something different.

I started talking. I explained to Dave how I was feeling, and how I was ashamed to be feeling it. I rambled on for about ten minutes, feeling guilty about rambling on and sure I was going to be told I was crazy. But when I stopped talking and took a deep breath, all I felt was love.

The next day I found myself a cozy coffee shop and sat down

to write a blog post. I wanted to share what I was learning. My thoughts flowed onto the page as my fingers found the keys. I wrote about my pattern of hiding and withdrawing when I was overwhelmed and about how I had found I could choose something different. I wrote about my experience the previous evening—how I had noticed myself withdrawing, and how at the end of the night I had reached out for support. A couple of hours and a thousand words later, my post was nearly complete. I paused for a moment and read over what I had written, and then concluded:

I can't say that I avoided feeling overwhelmed or disappointed, but by allowing myself to feel what I was feeling and by being vulnerable and speaking from my heart, I was able to subtract some loneliness and add a lot of love, and that is something I am pretty excited about.

We are served best not by getting over, hiding, or avoiding our emotions, but by living and loving through them. We are served by listening to our heart.

Although speaking from my heart is not a "fix," loving life and myself even when I am overwhelmed is something I am willing to try on a little more often.

Overwhelm Attacks Again

I thought I had won. I hadn't.

My goals were simply biding their time. A week later, they struck back with a fresh onslaught of overwhelm, even worse than the last. Over the next two weeks it intensified. The weight of the insurmountable mountain of everything I had to do was growing. I was running at top speed through recurring cycles of inspiration—overwhelm—crash, with little relief.

When I picked up the phone and dialed Bay's number for

Chapter 7

our weekly coaching session, the last week of January I had had it. I was exhausted.

As the phone rang I thought back to the blog post I had written earlier in the month about choosing something different when I was feeling overwhelmed.

"You come up with some stupid, sappy, ideas sometimes, Danielle." I thought. Anger flooded me. The thought of either accepting and feeling my overwhelm or sharing more of it with the people in my life did not appeal to me. I was sick of sappy. I wanted a fix.

I glared at the goals that were outlined in the weekly check-in form I had sent to Bay for our coaching call. They included running my first marathon on May 4, 2014; upping my sleep to seven hours a night by the end of March; decreasing my emotional eating to less than three times a week, also by the end of March; designing and facilitating a wellness challenge for lawyers for the middle of May; getting my first coaching client by the middle of March; completing the first draft of the book I had started writing to help lawyers create lives that they loved by the beginning of August; working two of my own legal files and completing an examination for discovery by the end of June; raising a substantial sum of money to support mental health awareness in BC by the middle of July; volunteering through the Access Pro Bono Society twice monthly to help increase access to justice in BC; and working enough hours at my law firm to meet my financial goal of increasing my earnings and savings by twenty-five percent.

"And those are only a fraction of what you are trying to accomplish this year!" I reminded myself.

I thought about some of my other goals: complete my AC training program, including doing the twenty-odd homework practices we were assigned each month; connect weekly with my AC buddy for the month; participate in AC team calls; have weekly breakfast meetings with my AC teammates living in Vancouver; run six days a week including a two-to-three-hour run on the weekends; spend time with Dave and his family and grow a deeper connection in our relationship; continue my weekly chats with Jamie at work; spend time with friends; regularly call friends and family in Manitoba; write a weekly blog post; learn to love my body; and prepare for a three-week trip to Brazil and Peru in April.

Oh, and transform my entire internal belief system and achieve inner peace.

"No pressure," my sarcastic mind went off, and then more bluntly: "You're an idiot, Danielle. You can't do all this."

I turned my mind back to my phone, which had now stopped ringing.

"Hello!" Bay's loving voice filled my ear.

"Hi Bay," I replied with forced levity, trying to disguise how defeated I was feeling.

"How are you doing?" she asked innocently, although I could tell I hadn't fooled her with my fake cheeriness. She could sense I was in a rough state.

"I'm alright." I replied, sullenly. "I'm just feeling a little overwhelmed still. I can't seem to figure out how to stop being so stressed out about everything I'm up to."

"Uh-huh" she replied. "I saw your check-in form and coaching request. What do you need right now?"

"I don't know …," I began. "You know that saying—you can do anything but not everything? I feel like I am trying to do both and that by trying to do everything I am going to end up not doing anything. My schedule is always booked solid—all with things I love, but I feel like I am not devoting enough time to each of them. I missed my good friend's birthday last

Chapter 7

week. I feel awful about that. I am not getting in the hours I want at work. I haven't written as much of my book as I wanted. I haven't done as many of my AC homework assignments as I wanted. I feel like it's all slowly piling up and eventually it will be too late to 'catch up' and I will fail to complete each of my projects. I can't handle that. I have been trying unsuccessfully to 'fix' this problem by either finding a way do it all, or finding a way to be okay with not doing some of it. It's not working. An alternative to this type of either-or thinking would be awesome."

We dug into it. Bay began asking me some questions about my relationship to goals and overwhelm but I wasn't wholeheartedly engaging with her questions. All I could feel was the mountain of to-dos heavy on my back. I kept coming back to the problem. I simply had too much to do and too little time. I was exhausted. I was trying to grab on to a different perspective but all I could muster was more whining and complaints.

Bay was not fazed by my tantrums. She continued to offer love and support and ask helpful questions. I continued to refuse to be open to different perspectives and responded with even more complaints.

About forty-five minutes in, I had just come up with a fresh long-winded tirade of grievances I was sure would convince Bay my situation was hopeless. But instead of buying my story and giving me a sympathy card, she paused.

"Why are you trying so hard to be overwhelmed?" she asked.

Now it was my turn to pause. Her words resonated.

"What do you mean?" I replied, still in my resistant toddler-state.

"It's like you have backed yourself into a corner and have begun lopping off your own limbs," she reflected, and then paused again to let the image sink in.

I took a deep breath and then let it go. It was true. I had backed myself into a corner. And I had effectively taken away any chance I might have at a fair fight. Not only that—I had set up this fight in the first place. I was making myself the victim of my own life. Anger again rose up my throat.

"Aaaaaarrghhhh! You mean I have to be responsible for my whole entire life?" I protested, but this time my whining was merely resistance.

I did not want to take responsibility for the fact that I had been the one to set my own goals, that I had been the one to fill my schedule to bursting, that I had been the one to interpret everything I was up to as overwhelming, and that I was the one who kept trying to pretend everything was perfect until it piled up to the point that I crashed. I didn't want all that stupid responsibility. I just wanted it to be easier.

But I couldn't go back. Once I had the awareness that I was making myself a victim and fighting my own life, I could no longer pretend it was all out of my control.

I took a couple deep breaths and felt some of the tension I had been holding fall away. If it wasn't out of my control, it was in my control: I could do something about it.

For the Love of Grit

"Why am I trying so hard to be overwhelmed?" The thought buzzed in my head long after I had hung up the phone with Bay and gone back to staring at my to-do list with (slightly less) resentment.

"Why have I turned my much-loved goals into 'have-tos' and 'shoulds'? I've created a wall of resistance to everything I love to do. I'm setting myself up to fail by fearing I will fail. It's crazy and I'm sick of it!"

I put my to-do list down on my desk, packed up my things, and got ready for a Friday evening out. The questions flitted in

Chapter 7

and out of my mind as I sipped on wine and caught up with a friend, but it wasn't until late that night as I drifted off to sleep that a light bulb went off. In my groggy state, I reached over to my phone and sent myself an email, which simply said: "Satisfaction is in the striving."

I completely forgot about it over the weekend, but it hit me hard when I arrived at work and checked my email a few days later. My resistance to being completely and fully present in my life was setting me up to fail at creating this life that I love.

On the bus home from work it sunk in even further. I had to embrace process; the messy grit. And so I did. Arriving home ten minutes later, I dumped all of my bags on the floor. I smiled. It felt good.

"I'll clean up later," I thought.

I ate some dinner then met up with a friend and went for a run. I bought some groceries. I returned home. As I opened the door, the pile on the floor made me smile again. "This is strange," I thought. "Whatever. I will leave it there for now."

I poured myself a glass of wine and sat down to write a blog post. I couldn't focus. I got up. I had a sudden desire to dump out the bags that made up the pile on my floor.

"You really are crazy," I thought. Then I giggled and proceeded to dump all the bags on the floor. Including my purse. It felt amazing.

"Life is messy," I thought, a grin still spread wide across my face. "My floor should be too."

"Life really is messy." I stopped.

Something about this thought hit me hard. I had always known life was messy, uncontrollable, and unpredictable in many ways but I realized that some part of me had refused to truly allow it. I put on some music and got out my paints. I wanted to make a mess. I needed to let out what I was feeling, and my thoughts were not yet formulated enough to write a blog post. And so I painted, with my fingers. An hour later, my hands were covered in multiple colours of paint and I was surrounded by poster boards smeared with the words "Life is Messy. Love it all." I was ready to write.

The words began flowing out of me. I described my frustration with my goals, and the evening experience I'd just had of embracing the messy side of life. I paused and looked around at the chaos that was my apartment. I giggled again and the remaining tension fell from my shoulders. I turned back to my keyboard.

I have been trying to put everything neatly into its place for as long as I can remember. It is rare that I take something on if I don't have a high degree of certainty about how it will go and what the outcome will be. I try with all my might to control every minute of everything I do. And I try to fix everything that does not end up going the way I plan. But the more I try to fix it, control it, and make it certain, the more I keep getting hit with the mess. It is as though life has been trying to remind me to stop trying so hard. Life will always be messy.

And I've continued fighting anyway. Although I don't want to admit it, I know I am destined to lose the battle. But maybe losing is not really a loss. I had a great night. Maybe letting go of control and embracing all this mess is really a win. A win for life, of course.

But isn't life why we are here? Why fight against it? Maybe we can be on the same team. Maybe it doesn't have to be a battle after all. Wouldn't that be the ultimate win!

So, Quit Already

Two weeks later I was sick, and sick of embracing the mess. I hadn't written my weekly blog post, and I was beating myself

Chapter 7

up terribly on top of the physical pain my sinus cold was inflicting. I wanted to quit, but I wasn't willing to give myself permission. To me quitting meant failure and I was much more comfortable suffering through, sacrificing wellbeing and sanity, than admitting defeat.

By the time I got off my weekly coaching call with Bay, I had admitted to myself that quitting didn't have to mean failure. Quitting could mean whatever I chose it to mean. Quitting could mean listening to my heart. Quitting could mean love. Quitting could mean courage. Quitting could mean fun. So I took back quitting, sat down in front of my lap top, and wrote:

Last week I didn't write a blog post. I felt like a quitter. But I didn't really choose to be a quitter. I quit with resignation. I chose it to mean defeat. My arguments were convincing. I have a cold … I am tired … I am uninspired … I can't find the motivation … I have no choice. I just can't write. I am weak. I am lazy. I am a Quitter.

What I refused to acknowledge at the time was what I really needed was sleep, tea, and a little self-love. And what my mind didn't say was I choose to listen, acknowledge, and accept what I need. I choose sleep. I choose tea. I choose a little self-love. I am courageous. I choose not to write a blog post. I choose to be a Quitter.

But wouldn't it have been amazing if I had!

By taking back quitting, we double our choices and eliminate defeat. For every option we had before, the opposite is now available. And every option that would have been failure is now success. And if one day I quit writing blog posts completely, or quit anything else in my life, I hope I will choose to quit it with gusto and love.

So if you are ever going to give up something, put something off, or change your mind, before making a list of "reasons why you have to" and "accepting defeat," look a little deeper, find the real reason why you want to or need to quit, acknowledge it, accept it, and give yourself permission to be a Quitter!

The Final Attack

Allowing myself the indulgence of not writing a blog post had been nice, but when my cold subsided and the next week's to-do list arrived, I couldn't bring myself to quit anything on it, at least not anything big. I still wanted to do it all and I was still overwhelmed. My battle with goals had become a war. Toward the end of February, I was starting to think that maybe my entire approach to goals needed to change.

The last weekend in February, I went to Victoria to visit one of the judges I had clerked for who remained a close mentor and friend. While there, I shared my goal-setting dilemma with her and received an interesting response. She shared with me, mixed in with some of the stories that make up her rich and fascinating life, that she had never set a goal, at least not in the sense of trying to define or attain success. This startled me, as she is one of the most successful people I know. She also told me something else that initially I found strange: she's always thought of herself as a tree.

As I let the conversation sink in over the next few days, it made more and more sense. Instead of being guided by a particular, predefined outcome for her life, she is guided by a deep sense of who she is. The words "groundedness, intuition, values," and "integrity" were constantly floating around in my mind. I thought with all these ingredients surely I could come up with a solution to my problem with goals.

I began talking my ideas over with a few friends and came up with an alternate universe. In this universe, I wouldn't have goals. I might have some short-term things that I would work on, but there would be no rigidity, no "I have to," "I should," or "by when?" My direction in life would instead be guided by principle, my values, and the things that are important to me. I would simply trust that my life will take on the course it is supposed to take, and I will end up where I am supposed to end up.

I thought I had it all figured out. I ran my alternate universe past Bay. After an hour of trying to convince her that I had figured out the solution to my goals (and my life), fielding her questions about what I was going to do with my current projects in this alternate world, and listening (a little grudgingly) to her suggestion that I may want to take a look at how I define the word "goal," I was no longer sure my solution was as simple as I had made it out to be.

When I got off that call, although I wasn't ready to give up on my idea, I could see that what I was trying to do was "fix" my problem. It was an all-or-nothing approach to goal setting. Either I have goals and rigidity and what I love turns into a "have-to," or I have no goals and lots of flexibility and I can enjoy the moment. I thought a little more about my alternate universe and how it would apply to each of my projects.

"Do I want to just throw the goals out the window? What about my marathon? It has a defined end date; a date by which my training will be complete and I will step out on the road and run forty-two kilometres. How could I eliminate the goal on that one?"

I was back where I started. Or was I? While I was not ready to let go of my goals, I also was not ready to let go of a more flexible approach to life, one in which I trust myself a little more to act on what is important to me, without having a schedule that only allows me three hours of free time a week.

All You Need Is Trees

"Yes," I thought. "Trees." Energy coursed through me as I sat down to write my weekly blog post. It was the first week of March and I had been in a full on war with goal setting for over two months. I knew it wasn't a solution, but I also wasn't really sure I wanted a solution any more. I could feel truth resonating through me.

"Trees. That's it," I thought. "Nothing more."

I had always liked trees—I used to sit outside at my parents' farm and draw trees when I was younger; I had loved having dinners in the field during harvest under the big oak tree at the top of the hill on the home quarter; on my trip to Africa two years earlier, out of all the amazing things I saw, some of the most beautiful were the trees; and there is really nothing better than climbing a tree, or hanging out under a tree with a good book, a notepad, or an iPod filled with songs.

Trees had been on my mind since returning from Victoria. They had come up in my journaling and in my conversations about goals with various teammates, friends, and mentors. My eyes would often drift to the big majestic limbs reaching toward the sky on my runs. I was doodling drawings of trees. I even started a painting of a tree with the intention of hanging it in my office. I didn't quite know what it all meant, or what I should be taking away from it.

As I was writing I realized I wasn't actually meant to know. Trees for me represent something big and mysterious; something incapable of being understood, fixed, or controlled. So instead of concluding my weekly blog post with a solution, I decided to write a poem.

Chapter 7

"A Tribute to Trees"

Grounded and billowing in the wind.
Taking a stand for time.
Secrets untold.
Weathered and worn, not weary; withstanding life's storms.
Solid, and filled with space.
Deep rooted and wild.
Stretching upward, outward, and deep within.
Source of Life. Air. Shelter. Beauty. Power.
Growing, renewing, and changing.
Swirling experiences ring upon ring.
Dancing playfully.
Telling a story with wisdom and grace.
Strength. Peaceful sage.
Whispering and creaking; leaves rustling in the wind.
Homely and shaded yet open and free.
Supporting. Supported.
Growing, reaching, twisting, inviting.
Enveloping and encapsulating each moment.
Connected and present, yet distant and aloof.
Wonder-filled darkness.
Untamed creativity and passion.
Tall, bent, fallen, and spikey.
Beacon of inspiration, of hope.
Rough, tough, and rooted.
Majestic and musical.
Young. Aged.
Timeless.
Limitless.
Alive.

But, How to Be a Tree?

The rain pounded on as my feet moved methodically over the wet pavement. The wind whipped across my face, piercing through my water-logged clothing and seeping deep into my bones. Waves crashed into the rocks below to my left, white peaks dancing in the waters that stretched out for miles.

"I can't go on," I thought as I turned my eyes back to the path in front of me and the sign that was approaching that read "Kilometre 35."

"Seven more kilometres in this will surely kill me."

Just then my shins began to spasm, requiring me to hobble sideways to catch my balance. Caught off guard and frustrated, I slowed to a walk. I hobble-walked a few more steps, feeling between the spikes of pain the edges of exhaustion threatening to shut down the throbbing muscles in my legs completely.

"Noooo! I will not quit now."

I thought back to a few weeks earlier when I had enthusiastically pulled on my shoes and headed out for a run at an altitude of three thousand feet. "Crazy lady," Dave had said with a mix of awe and affection when I returned an hour later with tales of breathtaking views in the hills surrounding Cusco, Peru. I had not trained as much as I would have liked in the month before my marathon, between nursing my shin splints and travelling through remote locations in Peru's mountain-thin air, but I had got in a few good runs.

More memories of the last month began flooding in, giving me strength. From trekking through Machu Picchu to sightseeing with a friend in Arequipa; from camping out in the middle of Lake Titicaca with the locals to savouring delicious meals in Lima; from staring out over the Colca Canyon into the eyes of a majestic condor to a weekend wedding in Brazil;

Chapter 7

and romantic dinners with Dave. My trip to Peru had been epic. It hadn't just been the fact that I had been able to check my Peru-trip goal off my list that had left me feeling pleased: every moment of the trip had been deeply satisfying in its own way. I suddenly felt grateful in every inch of me exactly where I was, standing tall and strong in the storm.

"You can do this, Danielle." I started running again, my frozen body warmed from the inside by my thoughts, my legs finding their methodical movement through the pain. One step, and then another, and then another—my feet made their way across the pavement, into the biting wind and rain around the far northwest corner of Stanley Park, back toward the city, past friends and supporters cheering me on, landing frozen and proud across the finish line. It was May 4, 2014 and I had just completed my first marathon.

Chapter 8—Body Love

The Rollercoaster of Recovery

It was more painful than I let anyone know. Although I had stopped purging my food, the battle waged on against my body. I was still bingeing a few times a week, and dealing with the discomfort and shame that followed. And I still did not like the way I looked. I desperately wanted to lose the fifteen pounds I had gained in the last three years. By health standards I was not overweight. I weighed approximately 135 pounds at five feet six inches. Yet I felt like a massive growing ball of lard. My stomach, which had for the first half of my twenties displayed the perfect hint of a six pack underneath a hard smooth exterior, had gone a little soft and lost its definition. My hips and thighs, which I'd always managed to keep from blossoming into their full hour-glass shape, were growing cellulose that I could see and jiggle. Although my size zero pants had long ago stopped fitting, I kept them around. They taunted, tormented, and shamed me, and at the same time gave me hope that someday I'd lose the weight in a healthy way and get back into them. I still wanted to be skinny.

For the most part, I hid my pain. I had stopped bingeing officially on Christmas Day 2013, although most people thought I had quit long before that. I was constantly giving people the impression that I was happier with my body and my recovery than I was. After letting out my secret that I had struggled with an eating disorder for eight years in January that year, I had gone into "but, I'm okay now" mode. For all of 2013, I had given the impression that I had recovered. I had been in recovery—consciously working on healing my relationship with food and my body, and consistently reducing the frequency of my purging—but I hadn't stopped yet. I wasn't recovered. And certainly the pain was still real.

When I vowed to myself on Christmas Day 2013 that I would never purge again, I knew it was a vow I would keep. The cost had simply become too high. I loved life too much to be spending it emptying my stomach over the toilet. It had been a huge milestone in my recovery, yet the days and months that followed, and even the moment of the decision itself, had been anticlimactic. I had not celebrated or marked the occasion in any way. I hadn't even told anyone because I had been pretty sure everyone thought that I had stopped long before. I was ashamed it had taken me so long to get to that point. My mind was constantly telling me that I should be further along by now. Even in recovery, I wasn't good enough.

In the years I was actively bingeing and purging, my life had been governed consciously by many rules, and unconsciously by many more. The overarching rules had been always "lose weight" and "do not let anyone know you are doing it, or how." My eating disorder had begun to develop in my first year of undergraduate studies as a diet. I had been 130 pounds and completely healthy when I graduated from high school. I was moving to a big city. My braces, acne, bad haircut, and too much makeup days were behind me. I was an adult. I wanted to be sexy. I could look like a supermodel if I wanted to, I had thought. It can't be that hard. I just have to set my mind to it. So I did.

I took it on as a kind of fun challenge. I began counting calories in and out. I added in an hour at the gym here and there, said no to dessert and dressings and second helpings, and skipped meals when no one would notice. Soon I was

Chapter 8

logging everything, reading packages religiously, and Googling the calorie count for every single thing that entered my body. I kept note paper with me throughout the day, adding up calories consumed, subtracting calories burned. My goal was to net less than a thousand calories per day. I prided myself on feeling hungry and not giving in to the urge. If I fell asleep with my stomach burning with hunger, I felt like I had won some heroic victory.

Within a few months, I could estimate with a good measure of accuracy the number of calories in every meal at my residence cafeteria and every snack in the cafés around campus. By Christmas, my clothes were falling off me. I had lost twenty pounds. My friends and family worried, but I reassured them it was just first-year nerves. I just don't like the cafeteria food, I would explain. Being away from home is hard. Some people gain twenty pounds their first year; some lose it. Don't worry about me; I'm fine.

By that time, I likely would have been diagnosed as anorexic, and I was beginning to flirt with bulimia. When I was around other people, I tried to eat normally so they wouldn't suspect anything, but it was torture to break my own restrictive rules. I couldn't stand the thought I might possibly intake more calories than I burned in a day. If I ate a rich meal my internal calorie-calculating compass would go into full on panic mode.

"You just ate eight hundred calories!" it would scream. "Plus you ate three hundred at breakfast! That's more than a full day's worth! And you have dinner later! What are you going to do now?"

I would strategize. My options were exercise, find a way to skip my next meal without it seeming odd to anyone, or purge the excess food. I initially tried to convince myself of a healthy option: a run or the gym. Over time, my willpower waned. More and more full meals with others turned into opportunities to indulge and then purge the damage done.

Within a few months, bingeing and purging became part of the challenge. Taking out of the equation the inevitable pain and shame that followed a purge, the whole thing was exhilarating. I loved having a secret, and I loved the positive attention I was getting for losing weight seemingly without effort.

By spring break of my first year of university, I had lost over thirty pounds. Hovering just under a hundred pounds, I hit my lowest-ever adult weight. It was around that time I received my first real health scare. In addition to eating less than a thousand calories a day and bingeing and purging regularly, I was also sleeping very poorly (averaging three or four hours a night) and drinking alcohol excessively at least three nights a week. In March 2005, I got a bladder infection. With everything else going on in my body, I did not recognize it until it turned into a kidney infection and landed me in the emergency room with excruciating back pain and then a stay in the hospital overnight.

A kidney infection shouldn't have been that serious. The doctor was suspicious and asked many questions about my health in general, but I was too ashamed to admit I was struggling with anything other than the kidney infection. I was shaken and terrified; for the first time I had seen a glimpse of the impact of the war I was waging against my body. I knew it could have been much worse. I'd watched videos and seen pictures online of the health effects of eating disorders. I knew they could be deadly. I decided to stop. I left the hospital promising myself that this whole weight-loss kick I had been on for the past seven months was over. But by that time I was addicted to my real-life thriller. My resolve lasted a couple of weeks before I was back to playing by the rules of my deadly game.

Chapter 8

Now recovered, nine years later, I still couldn't quite let go of the game. Only a different set of rules applied. Now I was supposed to be okay with my body and my weight. I was supposed to be able to eat normally, have a healthy exercise routine, and not be tormented by unrealistic expectations. I was allowed to gain a little bit of weight, but not let myself go completely. I still had to look good physically. I had to be confident in my recovery progress, especially around others so they wouldn't worry about me. I was not allowed to go backwards. I had to learn how to love my body just as it was, and I had to do it quickly, so I could finally lose this weight in a healthy way. I had to have the perfect recovery.

I still had a secret. I was hiding the fact that my recovery was far from perfect. In many ways, my life went on just as it had. Although I was proud that I was no longer purging my food, the early part of 2014 was filled with nearly as much shame as when I had been. I was still using food to numb my emotions and distract myself. I was bingeing regularly. I was repulsed by my body, especially the expanding breadth of my hips and thighs. I didn't want to be soft and curvy; I wanted to be toned and lean. I refused to buy myself new jeans that fit. It would have crushed me to see hard evidence of how much weight I'd gained in the form of the number on their tag. I stayed away from all form-fitting clothing. I threw out my scale. I shied away from pictures that would capture anything more than a headshot. I hid from full-length mirrors. I filled my closet with flowing dresses and myself with denial. I made sure the external world—and the internal world of my mind—would not see the form of my lower half.

I felt powerless about how I looked. I feared that if I tried to eat healthy and exercise, I would take it to an extreme and it would become unhealthy. I swung back and forth between trying to be conscious of what I ate and giving myself full permission to eat anything. I felt either too controlled or completely out of control.

People told me my body had wisdom and that it would tell me what it needed on a regular basis, and that if only I listened that everything would be easy: I would arrive at my own body's natural healthy weight; I would look and feel amazing.

I didn't trust my body to tell me what it needed. I resented people who were in touch with this so-called body wisdom. To me it felt like they were both telling me they were better than me and holding out false hope. I tried to sit still and listen. I couldn't hear anything that sounded like my body talking. All I could hear were debates and screaming matches in my head.

"Oh, my God, don't eat that entire chocolate bar! You are getting so fat! You just ate a piece of banana bread. Nobody needs that much sugar at once. You don't really want it anyway. Yes, you do. Don't deny yourself the craving. You know what happens when you restrict. It will build up and explode and you will binge and eat everything. Just eat the chocolate bar. This is how it is in recovery. It's better to gain weight than to be back bingeing and purging all the time. If you let yourself eat it, you'll want it less. Just take the rules off the table. Give yourself permission. That's a stupid strategy. You're just tricking yourself so you can eat all kinds of crap. Don't you know there are consequences? You're going to end up a giant blob. Can't you feel how tight your clothes are? Soon even your dresses won't fit. These chocolate bars add up. You are getting pretty disgusting."

One chocolate bar could be agony. Since listening to my body wasn't working, I tried my other handy tactic: ignore everything. Ignore that I was bingeing. Ignore that I was gaining weight. Ignore the arguments in my head and the never-ending desire

Chapter 8

to be skinny. Pretend I didn't care. That didn't work either. My attempts to ignore ultimately resulted in self-manipulation. I took on projects that would not focus on my weight, but secretly, I hoped, would have the side benefit of having me lose weight: yoga challenges; running a marathon; goals to do splits and handstands.

I was really well-practiced at convincing myself I wanted something as a cover for something else, and my sneakiness worked for a while. There were times when I could honestly say I was happy with my recovery so far and I didn't care I had gained a little weight. After a few months of pushing down my desire to be skinny while still secretly trying to fulfill it, I began feeling exhausted. I hated that I was still hiding.

That April, I did some work around my relationship with beautiful, powerful women in general, and again specifically, with my younger sister; I recognized that I was still to some degree comparing myself, and especially my expanding body, to my sister, to my female friends, and to women in the media. It's not like I didn't get along with my sister. We had what most people would call a great sisterly relationship. We talked on Skype every few weeks, and texted to keep up with what was going on in each other's lives. We travelled well together, shopped together, partied together, went for runs together, joked around, and played games. And it was not as though I didn't have good female friends. I had a large circle of friends I could call up to go out for dinner, drinks, or dancing, or on some creative adventure. And I had a few close friends I could call up even when I was struggling with something or feeling down. My relationships with my sister and my friends were growing deeper all the time. It was just that when my internal critic was running the show, my desire to compare would sneak in and have me withdraw or resent my relationships.

And so, I also did some more completion work around my body image—an area where my internal critic still had a relatively strong hold. As I let go of another layer of the shame I was holding on to about my body, I got to a more honest place and admitted to myself that I wanted to lose some weight. I gathered up my courage and, in one of our coaching calls, shared with Bay that I still secretly wanted to be skinny and that I wanted to feel like I had my power back around my own body image.

By the end of our call I had taken my weight back into my own hands. I began a healthy diet and exercise routine, and I asked Daniel, one of my AC teammates who lived in Vancouver, to be my accountability buddy. I started making progress. A little over a month later, I had lost five pounds. Then I cheated on my diet and gained two back. I began getting frustrated with the whole thing, partially because it wasn't sustainable and partially because something was still missing. The inner turmoil and pain hadn't disappeared. I had thought that quitting purging my food would make everything better. It hadn't. And, I was realizing, neither was losing weight the "healthy" way. The voices were still there, at least to some degree. I was discouraged. I began slipping back into my bingeing ways and letting my demon have its way.

Feeling the Feelings

I lay on my back on my couch, curtains drawn to the late Saturday morning sun, still feeling the effects of my food hangover from the night before.

"Why do you do this to yourself?"

The night before, a beautiful Friday evening in late May, I had turned down a number of social invitations on the premise

Chapter 8

of having a nice evening with myself. I had arrived home, poured myself a glass of wine and made myself a nice dinner. And then, instead of reading my book and enjoying a nice bath as I had planned, I had eaten a second helping of dinner even though I was not hungry, and slipped out to the restaurant a five-minute walk from my apartment to order take-out: a giant piece of chocolate cake with ice cream and two mammoth size cookies. I had snuck back into my apartment, poured myself an extra glass of wine and holed away, indulging in shame.

Now I stared at the ceiling, hands over my stomach wishing I could go back and undo what I'd done. My demon once again began its tirade.

"You pretend you are better but you aren't. You'll never get over this. You just can't control yourself. I don't know why you spend all this money on a personal development program. You're hopeless. Now you're just lying here feeling sorry for yourself. Why don't you at least get up and do something. It's almost noon. You're so lazy. You're useless. Disgusting."

Emotion threatened to overtake me. I tried to distract myself and push it down so I could get up and make a to-do list for the day, but the river was too strong. It was like a tidal wave pushing at my insides, pulsing louder and harder and making my heart begin to roar. I would have to feel it. I decided to let it come ... and did it ever. I cried for a solid hour. Half crying, half screaming, tormented sobs rocked my entire body. Tears came big and heavy, flowing down the side of my face in rivers making a pool of wet in my ears and overflowing onto the couch. My heart, so big and so full, had burst free of its prison, leaving my chest splayed open to the ceiling, paralyzed in pain. I felt raw and exposed. I placed my hands over my shaking chest as if to prevent my heart from being trampled on or taken from me completely. It only screamed louder. I willed myself to break free of my paralysis and sat up quickly thrashing my arms and pounding my fists on the couch in frustration, trying to shake out the pain and make it stop. My heart would not be silenced. Somewhat in awe and somewhat terrified at the power of my emotions, I let go and doubled over, sobbing in tear-soaked defeat.

In the wake of my cry, my world regained a measure of peace. I also realized the grief I was feeling was not for the state of the progress I had made in my recovery from bulimia, but for the state of my relationship with myself. In that hour, I had begun to let go of some of the pain I had been carrying around. I had let myself feel how deeply I had hurt myself and was still hurting myself with my hateful thoughts and actions.

Although the sadness was still there, I started to feel lighter. I noticed I had access to a measure of compassion for myself that had not been present before. I had let go of a lot of the shame around how I had been treating myself and my body. I wanted to be kind to myself. Instead of hiding out for the day or making myself busy as I had planned, I picked up the phone and reached out to Dave for some love and support, and then to Steve, one of my AC teammates from Vancouver.

Owning My Beauty

Once I started crying I couldn't stop. The pain was closer to the surface than it had ever been before. I had opened the door to healing some deep inner trauma and it could no longer be closed. Although I felt a deep sense of peace after every cry, within a few days or a week, the waves of grief would build again. For most of the next month, I felt like I was holding back a volcano of tears that was ready to explode at any time.

One particular day in late June, I was sitting at my desk at

Chapter 8

work tormenting myself for having eaten too much, yet again. I couldn't stand it. I was so sick of myself and this stupid coping mechanism. I felt a deep sense of disgust and despair. My internal critic was in full-blown attack mode. After about half an hour of beating myself up and holding in the tears, another thought came to me. "I could talk to someone. What if I didn't wait until I was better to get some love and support?"

My thoughts immediately went to my mentor a few offices down. Although I did not feel entirely comfortable letting him see me fighting back tears, I knew he would be supportive.

Before I could talk myself out of it, I walked down the hall to Jamie's office and knocked. The moment I started speaking, what I already knew was confirmed: Jamie's opinion of me wouldn't have changed one bit if I had eaten ten chocolate bars or even if I'd gone back to purging my food. After a few minutes of conversation, I gained some perspective. Suddenly, my having eaten too much wasn't a massive setback that meant I was a failure; my not being at peace with my body yet didn't feel like the end of the world; nothing was as significant as I had made it out to be. By the time I left his office, I was laughing. I felt lighter. I felt grateful. I was okay.

A few days later, I went out and did something I never thought I would do—I bought myself a new pair of jeans that fit me just as I was. With every layer of shame and grief that I had allowed myself to release over the month came a deeper sense of peace and willingness to own my beauty. My outward appearance began to transform with my inner one. A few weeks after I had admitted to my coach that I was still struggling with my relationship with my body, I had found the courage to cut my near-bum-length hair into a shoulder-length crop, with bangs. Now a few weeks and many tears later, I found the courage to slip into some form-fitting jeans. I no longer needed to hide.

I Am Enough

As I stood up in front of my AC teammates in Seattle the first weekend in July, reflecting on the personal transformation I had made so far, I was beaming. I felt proud of all the progress I had made in my business and in achieving my goals, but nothing could compare to the feeling I felt at a deeper place. My heart fluttered. A warm spark filled me from the inside. I was glowing.

I felt beautiful. Just as I was. Inside and out.

Chapter 9—A Sprinkle of Joy

The Epic Pyjama Party

"Danielle, you choose the next one."
"Come on. You must have at least one you can put on."
"Yeah, it doesn't matter. You can choose anything."
"No judgment. Come on."
The voices of my friends prodded me until I finally gave in.
"Okay, fine. You asked for it," I said, as I made my way over to the computer and entered in the search term "Spice Girls Wannabe."
My musical repertoire consisted mainly of my high school favourites—Spice Girls and Eminem. Not that I didn't listen to music. I loved music. I was just too busy to spend time listening to new music and memorizing artist and song names. My ignorance suited me fine most of the time as I liked most genres of music and was usually happy to turn jukebox control over to someone else. I was especially happy to turn control of the tunes over to any of the sweaty barefooted music lovers dancing around me.

We had retired to the home of a friend we were staying with for the weekend after a day of transformation in downtown Seattle. We enjoyed a delicious meal with a few of our teammates, before heading out to a live music show. All of us too alive and full of love to sleep, someone had turned on some music as we were getting ready for bed. Now half an hour later, we were in the midst of an epic kitchen dance party in our pyjamas.

This is how it was for Daniel, Steve, Scott, Steph, and me,

my AC teammates from Vancouver. Deep bonds of trust and love flowed among the inseparable five who had been strangers merely seven months before. Thrown into an intense coaching program where social niceties and maintaining an image were not part of the deal, we quickly got to know each other at a depth only attained after years of friendship. Add in a three-hour drive in a cherished blue van called Baby Blue or a cramped rental car to and from Seattle once a month, weekly 7:00 a.m. breakfasts, daily sharing on a private Facebook group, and frequent texts and calls, and you get the creation of the unstoppable force we called the Van City Coach Crew.

This evening of connection was one of many we had shared over the course of the year. While shared laughs, cries, conversations, and epic dance parties were not uncommon among our group, this night in particular was special for me. It was the night I got the first taste of something I'd lost long ago. As I was dancing and singing my heart out to "Wannabe" by the Spice Girls, a feeling began to rise from deep within. It started as a tingling, a warmth deep in my core that began to spread over my body like wildfire, filling me with a bright white light, melting my fears, melting my heart, melting my lips into a smile so wide I was unsure my face could contain it.

Joy. Beautiful full-bodied joy.

It was not as though happy feelings were unfamiliar to me. I was often joking around, being silly, laughing and smiling in all areas of my life—at work, in my romantic relationship, with friends and family, and on social media. You can find me giggling uncontrollably on at least a weekly basis. I was always creating something fun and exciting in my life.

This was different. It was expansive. It was rich. It was powerful. It was uninhibited. It had substance. It filled the deep crevices in my soul, seeping into every inch of my body and

Chapter 9

overflowing into the world. It reminded me of the free-flowing ecstasy you see in a child twirling round and round until she gets so dizzy she falls down in fits of giggles, jumping up and down on a mattress with unbounded glee, or dancing her heart out on an empty dance floor at a wedding. I was that child.

It had been a long time since I'd felt this depth of joy. It was a mark of the deep trust we had created among the five of us that I had allowed myself to sink into this freedom. It felt safe to let out my five-year-old self, and in that safety I found delicious, exquisite joy. My comfort with my sweaty dance mates was one factor that allowed me this new level of joy. The most significant reason for this new depth of expression was my own comfort level with myself. Over the past month, I had let myself feel painful emotions of grief, shame, and anger more deeply than ever before. I was learning firsthand that often-spoken truth that when you limit one end of the emotional spectrum you limit its opposite to an equal extent. By owning my shame, I began to own my beauty. By allowing my grief and anger, I had now attained a state of unreserved love and joy. I couldn't remember the last time life felt so good.

A Summer of Exciting Challenges

My new-found joy was not the only exciting thing bubbling up in the summer of 2014. As was becoming my new normal, I took on a number of exciting adventures and challenges to push my comfort zone and fill my adrenaline cup.

The first was a wellness challenge I organized with other members of the Young Lawyer's group I was a part of, for all members of the legal profession in BC. My excitement shone through in the blog post I wrote to entice all members of the legal profession to join.

Calling All Members of the Legal Profession—CBABC Young Lawyers Have a Challenge for You!

I am the Wellness Officer on the CBABC Young Lawyers executive and a member of the section's wellness committee. I am writing this post to invite you all to join our 10-Day Wellness Challenge that starts today, June 23, 2014, and runs until July 4, 2014!

You can sign up and join in at www.wellnessinbrief.org. More information about the challenge is set out below, and on the Wellness Challenge website.

Wellness Challenge 2014

Do you have a wellness goal? Is it to dust off that bike and get outside to enjoy the sunshine, or to complete a road race? Perhaps it's to finally attend that yoga class you've been dying to try? Maybe it's to cook that delicious recipe you found instead of ordering take-out from where they already know your usual order?

Share your wellness achievements with your colleagues and challenge them to be well too!

The CBABC Young Lawyers Lower Mainland Section Wellness Committee challenges you to be well! We are encouraging all members of the legal profession—paralegals, support staff, lawyers of all ages, judges, court staff, etc.—to dedicate some time to wellness in any area of your life, not just health, each weekday for two weeks.

Register now at www.wellnessinbrief.org!

Dedicate some time to wellness (in any area of your life, not just

Chapter 9

health) each weekday for two weeks and share your experience by:

- Facebook—tagging and posting to the Canadian Bar Association
- Twitter—tweet us at @CBA_BC and use #wellnessinbrief and the day of the Wellness Challenge that you've completed (e.g. #WCDay1, #WCDay2 etc.)
- Instagram—share your photos with us using hashtag #wellnessinbrief and the day of the Wellness Challenge that you completed it on (e.g. #WCDay1, WCDay2 etc.)
- You get one wellness point for each day that you post. We hope you will join in, be creative, and get a little excited about treating yourself well!

The second adventure was a personal challenge, and spoke to the daredevil in me. On June 22, 2014, I rappelled down the Hyatt Regency Vancouver (which is 358 feet high) in support of the Make-A-Wish Foundation.

The third was a move. While down in Peru, Dave and I had reached a new level of trust and intimacy in our relationship. We decided we would take the next step of moving in together when my lease came up in July. One week of packing and an awkward experience with a moving van that was at least twice the size we required later, we were surrounded by boxes in our new home and life together.

The fourth was a four-day adventure down to Portland, Oregon for World Domination Summit (WDS), an annual conference for community-minded entrepreneurs. Between inspiring speeches at the conference, fun meetups and events, meeting Scott Dinsmore and the Live Your Legend community, and parties that featured hot air balloons at night, WDS was a blast.

The fifth was a planned surprise. At a networking event I met a lawyer who was starting a surprise-event planning business. I thought it was a brilliant idea. As part of promoting her new business she offered to plan a free surprise-event date for me to surprise Dave with, in exchange for testimonials and doing a little write up for her blog afterwards. The date went off without a hitch. We participated in duelling lessons and learned how to attack each other with old-fashioned swords. When we returned home to change out of our duelling clothes before supposedly heading out to a restaurant, Dave was impressed to find our balcony had been set up for a romantic dinner in. It was a beautiful night.

The sixth was a ten-day spoken word poetry challenge that I called "Suits and Capes" where I, you guessed it, dressed up in a suit, put on a cape, and performed a spoken-word poem that I had written. For two weeks I nervously stood in front of my web cam and spoke my heart out to the world of YouTube and Facebook. It was terrifying and fun!

So much joy, love, and excitement. What a summer it was.

Chapter 10—The Big Guns

Money Madness

The phrase "client game"—often used in my coaching program to describe the process of generating clients—made my blood boil. Coming up with a strategy to fill my pipeline with potential clients, provide a sample session, and get someone to sign up with me was not fun in my books. Don't get me wrong. The sample session was almost always fun, and usually so was the conversation before that in which I offered that sample session. The part I hated was the conversation that included me telling the potential client how much I charged, asking if they wanted to work with me, and coaching them through any objections (with their permission).

It was mostly my wacky feelings about money and my fear of asking for anything in return for my coaching services that had me adamantly denying that I wanted to be a coach for the first six or so months of my AC program.

"I signed up for this program for the personal growth and leadership training," I would say. "I don't want to be a coach." This was weird because I had used the word "coach" to describe myself on my first TYS business cards in early 2013 and I had started offering stress-busting coaching services to young lawyers later that year.

The truth is I simply wasn't good at separating my own personal worth from the service I was offering. I put so much of myself on the table when I asked someone to hire me that if they said no it hurt as if they had told me I was a useless excuse for a human being. I struggled with how to be committed to getting clients instead of the two extremes of getting attached to making everyone I spoke to become my client or not trying at all. Committed nonattachment, I was realizing, is a tricky edge to play. So although I was coaching my teammates all the time (and enjoying it) and was being coached (and getting a lot of value from that) for the first few months of my coaching program, I decided I simply didn't really like offering life coaching to others.

The thing that had me begin to change my tune was getting my first client. She was a big dreamer with an even bigger heart and tons of fiery courage. I loved working with her. It felt wonderful to stand for her greatness and to hold a safe space for her to process her internal world and overcome her fears. And it was fun!

The second thing that cracked me open a little further was attending WDS at the beginning of July. In the four days I was there, I met many inspiring entrepreneurs who got me excited about building a business, and I left with the contact information of a number of people interested in a sample coaching session with me. When I came back I was on fire.

This led me to the third thing that cracked me right open into a gooey pool of coach love: getting my second coaching client. He was a big dreamer with a kind heart who lived for the journey. I loved working with him! In one of our first coaching sessions he came up with a beautiful vision for the love relationship he wanted to create in his life; it was so powerful that it moved me to tears. I am happy to report that not two weeks later he met that woman and they are now happily married.

In late July, I was riding high on inspiration, and ready to own that I wanted to be a life coach. A week later I got my chance to state that ownership. I was in Seattle at my coaching program weekend. We were making our monthly client game declarations. This had, up until then, been my least favourite part of the weekend; the part where we went around the room sharing struggles we were having building our coaching practice, asking for support, and declaring to the group how many clients we would generate in the upcoming month. It was meant to make business-building fun and supportive. I resisted it to the max. I treated it like something vile *they* were forcing me to do and responded to all attempts to get me excited with, "I don't really want to be a coach anyway." This month was different.

When it came to be my turn I enthusiastically declared my clients for the month and proceeded to make my first passionate speech. Speaking from a place of leadership that I did not know I possessed, I shared my story of how I got my second client by simply showing up as myself, instead of looking for validation and, catching myself even more off-guard, I began to enroll my team in how easy and fun getting coaching clients could be. *What?*

When we all stood up at the end of the weekend to make our usual declaration and commitment to being a coach and leader and part of the team to the end of the year, I wholeheartedly meant every word.

Integrity Insecurities

I must have seen into the future and known that I would fall in love with coaching as I had taken my website offline at the beginning of July for "some serious reinvention." By mid-August, TYS was back online with a new logo and vision. My site was looking good! My vision had expanded to not only include reinvention of the legal profession and helping lawyers trash their stress, but the possibility of reinvention everywhere: a world where everyone gets to create a life that they love.

I Am Enough

Mission

TYS's mission is reinvention in service of creating lives that we LOVE.
TYS's mission is to make impossible things happen.

Declarations

I declare that change is not enough; it is time for reinvention.

I declare that to live lives that we LOVE we must reinvent the way we are being.

I declare that to reinvent our profession we must first reinvent ourselves and the way we are being.

I declare the possibility that what is possible is what we say is possible.

Commitments

I am committed to standing for the possibility of making impossible things happen.

I am committed to standing for the possibility of reinvention.

I am committed to standing for the greatness of human beings.

I am committed to standing for the possibility of creating lives that we LOVE.

I am committed to reinventing myself and the way I am being.

I am committed to vulnerability and speaking my truth boldly.

I am committed to strength in the face of resistance.

I am committed to creating a life that I LOVE.

Call Forward

Reinvent yourself. Reinvent your work. Reinvent your life.
Step into your greatness. Create a Life You LOVE.

Chapter 10

I was committed to being a coach and a leader. I was committed to reinvention. I was committed to creating a life that I love. I was committed to helping others to reinvent their lives and create lives that they love. I was inspired and ready to take on my new vision for the world. Wasn't I?

Within a few weeks, the excitement of getting a new client began to fade and I became busy with legal work, leaving my efforts to build my coaching practice under a pile of documents in the corner of my office. "What am I really committed to?" This was the question I faced as I watched my actions move farther away from the beautiful vision I had created for my business a month earlier.

"Does being a great coach and leader leave room for me to be a lawyer? Am I committed to creating a legal practice? Am I really committed to being a coach? Did I just get excited because I got a new client? Am I really committed to anything that I am up to?" By the end of August my mind was filled with doubts.

A week into September I was at one of my favourite cafés, where I had been settled in for a few hours across the table from Scott, a teammate from my coaching program and member of the Van City Coach Crew. I had been working on my book and he on his PhD dissertation. After a few hours of work, we had gradually transitioned to sharing our struggles, coaching each other, and contemplating life. I had just finished telling him about my struggles with choosing a career path and being committed to it.

Scott asked if I wanted to hear what he saw for me. The tone of his question made me nervous, and I had a sense that I might not like the reflection he was offering to share, but I did want to hear it. I was in a year-long coaching program after all and by this time I knew that the most powerful reflections were usually the ones that challenged us, and that we didn't really want to hear. I told him I wanted to hear what he saw. He reflected that I often showed up very inspired and passionate and then I disappeared, and that I do this everywhere in my life. He said my enthusiasm felt ungrounded—over the top inspiration and passion, and then I was gone—the impact being that although I take on big inspiring things and my enthusiasm can be contagious, it is hard to continue to be inspired by me long term, and it's hard to know what's real.

My breath caught in my chest. Emotions swirled inside me: first anger, then fear, then sadness and defeat. I knew it was true. I was constantly coming up with new exciting ideas to convince *myself* to get back on my own roller coaster every time I crashed it. I could see that I often did show up in short bursts of inspiration (like the two-week spoken word poetry challenge I had just completed in August) and then quickly disappeared (like the past two weeks when I had generated no newsletter or blog post at all).

"Am I committed to all of what I say I'm creating ... or am I really only committed to the appearance of it? Am I trying to achieve my dreams through excitement alone?" The thoughts continued to torment me long after Scott and I had said goodbye and I had made my way home.

As difficult as it was for me to admit, once I had accepted the truth I saw in the pattern he reflected, I started to feel more empowered. I could do something about this. I immediately began trying to figure it out. "Why did I take on new things with such conviction, only to find myself a short while later out of integrity with my commitments? Why was I always all in and then out, in and then out?"

What I realized as I began to write a blog post about it a few days later is that my wavering commitment was often driven by

Chapter 10

a deep underlying fear that I am not enough. Acting on inspiration without committing gave me an easy out for when I would fail (because if I'm not good enough I am of course doomed to fail) while my bursts of excitement made it seem like I was perfect and "all in."

"What I am really committed to is maintaining appearances," my internal critic chimed in as my fingers moved over the keys. "So, of course, the result is it's hard to continue to be inspired by me and it's hard to know what's real."

While I knew my internal critic's conclusion was not completely out to lunch on this one, I also knew it wasn't the whole story. I knew I wouldn't have been writing a blog post about my struggles with integrity if I was really only committed to appearances. I pushed send on my post and promised myself this was not the end. I would figure this out.

Commitment Confusion

The next week, I had had enough of not knowing. I wanted to know myself as being committed. So on the evening of September 16 as I was going to bed I wrote a declaration on a paper: "September 17, 2014—Create a breakthrough in committing to my career." Like clockwork, an answer showed up shortly after midnight, in the form of a resonating thought: "Commitment must begin within."

I wrote it down, stared up at the ceiling and waited. The thought repeated again, and then again. "Commitment must begin within." I didn't quite get it yet, but it felt right.

I looked over at Dave already asleep beside me and then back up at the ceiling.

"Commitment must begin within." I underlined what I had written on the notepaper, and when nothing more fell into place, I curled back up on my side.

"I'll figure it out in the morning," I told myself as I drifted off to sleep.

The next morning the significance of the sentence began to fall into place. "Unless there is an underlying commitment to something within my power," I thought, "trying to commit to something outside myself will result in attachment to outcome and my choices not being good enough."

I thought about my commitment in my romantic relationship. "In the past I have always tried to be committed to something outside myself (a guy, a relationship, or the appearance of something) and my romantic relationships have never really worked. There was always a lot of drama. I was either attached to the outcome (completely in love and wanting to get married) or heart closed and resigned (doubting whether I'd found the right guy or the right relationship and keeping one foot out the door).

"This time," I thought, "things are different with Dave. And that is because my commitment first started within. I became clear on the things that I want to create and experience in a romantic relationship—the big ones being love and partnership—and I committed to them first. Once I knew it was in my power to create those things in my life, I no longer had doubts. The pressure to find the right guy and the perfect relationship was replaced by the freedom to choose the guy and the relationship that I would empower to create with me the things I am already committed to creating.

"I still had to find an amazing guy who was committed to creating and experiencing those things with me in order for it to work," I reminded myself, "but it became so much easier to find that person when I owned my power to create and experience the things I wanted. Once I committed at that deeper level within myself, I found that guy was already right there."

Chapter 10

"The more I became aware of what I wanted," I thought, "and held myself as powerful enough to create and experience it, the more I was able to empower someone else to help me create and experience what I wanted. Only when I was enough did it become possible for someone else to be enough."

I smiled as my thoughts turned to the question of how I might apply this formula to my career. I could see that I had been trying to commit to an activity or a career path—a thing outside myself. I had not yet fully identified what I wanted in the area of my life called "career" at a deeper level, or owned it as within my power to create and experience. And so, I had been either attached or resigned to how my career went; getting really inspired and then doubting whether I had chosen the right path. Ultimately, I had set myself up because no path would ever be good enough.

I looked a little deeper within. "What do I really want to create and experience in my career?" I asked myself.

It was obvious. I wanted to make a difference. I pulled out a pad of paper and wrote it down. "I want to make a difference. I want to make a difference in the lives of individual people in my life. I want to make a difference in my profession. I want to make a difference in the world. I want to make a contribution.

"It is easy to commit to making a contribution," I thought. "And I know that making a contribution is something that is within my power to create and experience."

Of course, in order to create and experience what I wanted, I still had to choose something external to commit to, but the choice was now a freedom, not a burden. "I have the freedom to choose to commit to law or coaching or writing or speaking, or all of them, or something else completely," I laughed to myself. "No matter what I choose, as long as I allow it to be the vehicle through which I make a contribution it will be enough. The path will be right because I allow it to be so!"

And then just as with my relationship, the thing outside myself I wanted to choose was already there.

"I choose all of it! In service of my commitment to contribution, I choose to commit to all that I am up to—writing, practising law, speaking, and coaching. All of these things will allow me to make a contribution."

As I sat back in my chair and reviewed my notes, I felt a sense of satisfaction. I knew it would not be easy to consistently practise commitment from this deeper place, and that I would sometimes slip back into attachment or doubt, but I could never go back from this awareness.

"I am enough, and so are all of the things I have chosen to be part of my life." I thought. "I have finally figured this commitment thing out."

I smiled as I sat down to share what I had learned in my latest blog post.

Chapter 11—The Significance of Time

Getting Over Myself

I was sitting at my desk paralyzed with how much I had to do. Half an hour earlier as my mind had been racing from thing to thing, I had stopped kidding myself that I was being productive and put aside the legal work I had been attempting to do. I had taken out a pad of paper and a pen and written everything into a nice organized to-do list. I had thought it would help me focus. Now that I had finished, I was just staring at it completely paralyzed.

It was mid-October, one month after declaring I was committed to everything, and I found myself behind on everything—from law work to AC homework, from building my coaching practice to writing blog posts, from buying groceries to doing laundry. I had social engagements scheduled every evening of the week, and support calls with my AC team booked in throughout every day. I hadn't been getting enough sleep for the past few days, my productivity was dwindling, and my reliance on coping mechanisms was increasing. I looked over at the empty chocolate bar wrapper beside me, evidence of my indulgent avoidance only moments before. I wanted to scream at the top of my lungs, or cry, or both. I felt like everything was coming to a head. I wanted to give up.

"Go for a walk, Danielle," another voice said. I knew it was a smart idea. I stood up, put on my coat, and walked out of my office toward the elevators. As the elevator doors opened and I stepped in, a vivid memory from a year earlier arrived front and centre in my mind.

I Am Enough

I had been on my way home after a long day of work.

My hands moved frantically through the collection of small objects at the bottom of my purse—old bus tickets, hairpins, pens, lip chap, an elastic bound stack of business cards of people I'd been meaning to follow up with. My wallet, umbrella, and other larger items had already been removed and placed on my lap for better access.

"How could it not be here?" I wondered for at least the tenth time. "It had to be. I would not have left the office without it." My hands again moved automatically to my outer jacket pockets and then my suit jacket pockets, my mind demanding my fingers to continue their search, unwilling to believe what my heart had known three blocks before. I had already searched my purse and all of my pockets thoroughly at least five times.

I glanced out the bus window toward the quickly disappearing tower now almost six blocks behind, as if staring at it might somehow summon my cell phone from the desk where it lay charging in an office on the twentieth floor.

"You left your phone at work."

The moment my mind accepted the fact, I instantly felt compelled to get off the bus and go back for it. As I stood up to push the button that would indicate to the bus driver I wanted to get off at the next stop, the items on my lap fell to the ground. Thoughts swirled in my mind as I bent down to retrieve my possessions from the bus floor.

"How could I survive a night without it? What if someone was trying to get hold of me? What if something came up that I needed to deal with? I have to go back for it."

Items safely stored in my purse once more, I stood again to reach for the stop button, but this time I stopped myself. Different questions had joined the swirl in my head.

"Who said I needed to be available and on demand all the time? What could possibly be so important that it can't wait until tomorrow?"

Chapter 11

Half standing, half sitting, arm stretched half way out in front of me I realized the answers to those questions were "I did" and "nothing." The bus came to a quick stop at a red light and I lurched forward and fell sideways onto the seat beside me.

Collecting myself, I tried to think it through rationally. It was nearly 7:00 p.m. I didn't have any plans for the evening that would require me to communicate with people using my cell phone. I was simply going home to make dinner, maybe write a blog post or go for a walk, and relax. My laptop was at home. I could email or Facebook someone if I needed to. There was nothing that couldn't wait until tomorrow.

"Everything can wait until tomorrow." I repeated the admission to myself.

For a moment I felt relieved that I wouldn't have to go back for my cell phone, and then, surprisingly, I felt disappointed. I tried to ignore the feeling, but I didn't have my phone or anything else to distract myself with. As I was forced to sit there with the uncomfortable emotion, I tried to think of something that might be urgent at work or of plans with friends I could make that would justify going back for my phone. I cursed myself for dropping my stuff and the bus for jolting me, causing me to stop and rethink my initial automatic decision to go back.

"I would be much more comfortable with my phone," I thought.

After a few moments of trying to manufacture urgency so I could go back for my phone and avoid the discomfort, I gathered my strength and began to explore it.

"What is causing this disappointment?" I asked myself in a whisper. After a few moments of resistance, during which I could feel my entire body frantically and repeatedly trying, without success, to grab on to anything that would distract me, I got the answer to my question, in the form of a question. "If nothing is urgent, does that mean the things I have taken on really aren't important?

"What if no one ever really needs me? Maybe I'm actually dispensable," the answer continued. My stomach continued writhing, as if trying to save me from the pain of the realization I was having. "I wanted to have to go back for my cell phone, because I want to feel needed. This whole thing is about fear. Fear of being dispensable and unimportant."

I was as uncomfortable with the shame I felt at having such a fear as I was with the fear itself. "No wonder I was trying to distract myself so much," I thought. After a few moments I pulled myself out of the shame spiral and tried to see the whole thing in a lighter note. Although the discomfort at not having my cell phone was still there to some degree, a few blocks later I was chuckling to myself about the irrationality of my fear. I pushed the stop button, this time preparing to get off at my own stop, and sat back down and breathed.

As I walked up the steps to my apartment a few moments later, I started thinking about how this fear of not being important might be at play on a bigger scale.

"How often do I manufacture unnecessary urgency? How often do lawyers in general manufacture urgency? Is it possible we convince ourselves that the things we are doing are much more important than they really are? Maybe we all just need to get over ourselves a little."

The elevator doors opened once again and I pulled myself back into the present as I stepped into the lobby.

Hot anger welled up in my gut as I considered the possibility that I was simply giving things too much significance, and that I might need to get over myself a little. The urgency of everything felt so real. Things had been piling up for weeks and I didn't know how to let go.

"When will I finally be over this?" I thought as I began walking toward the street in front of my office building, tears threatening to overtake me.

Chapter 11

Admitting Defeat

Five minutes later I was having a breakdown in downtown Vancouver on the corner of Seymour and Georgia Streets. I was crouched into myself on the sidewalk crying my eyes out. It was early afternoon on a weekday; cars whizzed past me a few feet away and people walked around me uncomfortably averting their eyes. I didn't care. I was so sick and tired of this stupid pattern of getting overwhelmed, not sleeping enough, and hating myself when I didn't get enough done.

"When will I finally be over this?" I thought again through my tears.

When I was growing up, my family had always been of the mind that it's better to have too much to do, than too little. "Stay busy to stay out of trouble" and "you'll go crazy if you have nothing to do" were two common sentiments in our household. My parents were both hardworking and ambitious, starting a hog farm from the ground up—taking on loans, hiring contractors, building barns and filling them with smelly pigs, making business connections, shipping the hogs to market, doing the accounting, and getting their hands dirty in the day-to-day operation of the barn. They grew the business from the spark of an idea into a profitable three thousand hog operation.

My mom, also a teacher and an artist, was always encouraging my siblings and me to learn something new. By the time I began kindergarten at age four I could speak both French and English and work with letters and numbers. I had also made many paintings and drawings, and creations with clay. My dad, also a mechanic and high-pressure welder, taught us how to fix things and work with our hands. My parents signed my sister and me up for all the different activities in the area, including swimming, figure skating, ballet, gymnastics, 4-H, and piano, letting us try them out and continue with the ones we enjoyed. Our activities were balanced with helping to take care of our little brother; helping out with chores in the barn, farm yard, garden, and house; and with all kinds of play—cards, board games, puzzles, tree forts, tobogganing, camping, cross-country skiing, dress up, make believe, and visiting friends and cousins.

Our lives were full, but not in an overwhelming stressful kind of way. We were just always occupied with something. It was when I was eleven or twelve, about the same time I found myself losing popularity among my peers in junior high, when my time issues began to inflame. My response to being rejected or feeling like I was not good enough had always been to prove them wrong—to "do more," "be better," and "try harder." But I hadn't had too much rejection up to that point in my life. And so my perfectionist tendencies had remained a mild undercurrent: winning me awards and praise and approval from my parents, teachers, and coaches (and friends until then), but not really causing me much harm. At the first hint of rejection, my perfectionist strategies intensified. I began agonizing over every conversation, every outfit, every task, every assignment, every activity. I took on more and I perfected to a higher and higher degree everything I did and everything I said in the hopes that one day I would prove to my friends (and to the world and myself) that I was good enough.

My mind began its incessant chatter as a natural response to the stress of perfecting everything, and it was then that my sleep issues began. I remember many nights in my pre-teens sneaking into the next room and tormenting my sister (who had always been a great sleeper) with deep conversations and puzzle books until 2:00 a.m. By my undergrad years, I was sleeping three or four hours on a good night. Many nights my

Chapter 11

heart would not stop racing the entire way through as I tried in vain to count sheep, and instead counted the to-do items I had not yet checked off and the excess calories I had consumed. I stewed over things I had said or done and I planned out my perfect tomorrow.

I was prescribed sleeping pills after a couple of weeks of being able to count my total hours of sleep for the week on two hands. That helped for a week or two, until my mind found a way to overpower the medicine and I started having to take a full pill instead of a half, and then two instead of one. I was scared of becoming addicted. And I hated the sleeping pills anyway. They made my mouth taste like acid in the morning. So after a few months I cut them out and went back to my midnight critique.

All through law school, clerking, articling, and my first six months as an associate, I continued to struggle with having too little time and getting too little sleep. I was just never able to fit in everything I had on my plate. When I started out on my mission to fill the void in January 2013, figuring out how to de-stress during the day and fall asleep at night were high on my list of priorities. And I made some good progress. By mid-2014, I was consistently sleeping between six and seven hours a night and I was way less stressed out about the calories I consumed and the things I achieved.

But my stress and sleep issues weren't completely resolved. Although the battles were less extreme, my relationship with time was still filled with strife.

About half way through my AC program my teammates and I had distinguished our relationship with time in what we called an "overwhelm cycle." It was similar to the pattern Bay and I had identified early in the year where I would get really excited about a bunch of new goals; set impossible expectations; start taking action really excitedly; fail to meet one of my impossible expectations; pretend it's fine and try harder; cut out sleep and self-care; feel more and more exhausted and overwhelmed; withdraw, crash, and feel like a failure; get some kind of support and inspiration; and then repeat the whole thing again. As I sat, crouched and crying on a busy street in broad daylight on that October afternoon, I knew exactly where I was in my pattern: crashing and feeling like a failure. I had been at this point a million times before and I was completely fed up with the whole pattern to the point of exhaustion.

After wallowing for another five minutes, I decided to call one of my coaching teammates to get some support. Although part of me really just wanted a friend to give me some sympathy, I decided to call my teammate Aubrey, because her bold coaching style scared me a little and I knew she would be able to coach me through this. Although coaching might not feel as nice as sympathy, I knew it would ultimately be more empowering.

I was right. Aubrey essentially told me to stop being such a whiney baby and to realize I was making it all up anyway so I might as well choose something different. She used nicer words than those and said it with love and prefaced it with, "Can I offer you a reflection?" But all I heard was "stop being such a whiney baby."

I had thought I was ready to hear the truth. I was, ultimately. But for a solid thirty seconds I became stone silent, my blood boiled, and my whiney-baby-self wanted to punch her in the face. After I collected myself enough to not scream "You're the whiney baby!" into the phone and hang up, I thanked her for her reflection, got off the phone and let the impact of her words sink in. It felt true. I was being a whiney baby. I was making it all up.

"By overscheduling myself, I set myself up to not have

Chapter 11

enough time every day." I thought. "And then, I spend a lot of time having breakdowns about not having enough time. I have another way of being—trees. But I am choosing not to be that way. I am creating a problem, probably because I am actually getting something from having a problem ... but what?

"Of course," my thoughts again returned to my overwhelm cycle. "I only allow myself to slow down and get some support when I have a breakdown or a problem, or when I'm feeling sad or broken or not good enough. I really just want a problem so that I can get some comfort and connection."

I already knew this sneaky little trick I played on myself quite well. One of the first things we had done early in the year in my AC program was to become familiar with our survival mechanisms (the default strategies we use in life that have gotten us to where we are). Mine were:

- Lazy Locomotive: high levels of action striving for some perfect standard, crashing, and repeating the cycle;
- Raging Buddha: denying, ignoring, or numbing my emotions, and putting on a calm exterior; and
- Precarious Princess: pretending I am fine and showing up put together when I am really about to fall apart.

I had discovered early on that my survival mechanisms operated together to ensure I only got support, love, and connection either when I was praised for being perfect, or things got bad enough that I finally crashed and allowed someone to see my emotions behind my mask of perfection. Although I had been working on allowing myself to be seen and asking for help from a more empowered place, my survival mechanisms still held a stronghold in key areas of my life. Time was one of them.

"My whole relationship to time is a strategy to get love and connection."

The thought hit me like a ton of bricks. Bay and I had often discussed my time issues in our coaching sessions, and I knew that they showed up in direct proportion to the significance I gave to things. I often gave external achievement or the praise and approval of others so much significance that it was overwhelming and excruciating when I didn't complete a task perfectly or in the time I had given myself to do it. And what I was realizing now was that the significance I gave to things was actually part of my strategy to fill the void.

"I make myself so busy that I will necessarily fail at completing it all," I thought, "so that I can have a problem, feel sorry for myself, and get some love and connection—both in the form of a much-needed rest and the comforting words of others. I make myself overwhelmed and stressed out in order to get love, both from myself and others."

My whole body resonated with the truth of what I'd just realized.

I sat down on the curb again feeling a mix of amazement and defeat. After a few minutes, my mind continued.

"But isn't it a flawed strategy? Is receiving love really contingent on my being either perfect or broken? What if I am already connected? What if I can't not be loved?"

Chapter 12—Owning What I Want

Passion Takes the Reigns

Sitting at my desk, I could not focus. I could not ignore the internal pressure any longer. It had been building for too long; the creative energy I had been suppressing was ready to burst. I set the legal file I had been working on to the side, pulled up a blank Word document, took a deep breath and set my fingers over the keys.

I have not been here in a while. It feels foreign. I am an imposter in someone else's space.

This place used to feel like home to me. I lived here week after week, pouring my story fiercely into the soft clicking keys.

Where did I go? I often wonder. And I haven't a clear answer.

And now, today, I have arrived. Unplanned. Caught off guard. Legal work left unfinished on my desk. I feel called to write, yet I have no particular story I want to share.

There is a beauty in extracting a piece of my heart and watching it flutter out into the depths of cyberspace. I have been longing for that. And yet I stay away.

My fingers ache for the keys. But my mind tells stories of suffering. My hands clench and pull away at the thought of sitting down and allowing the electricity to flow out of me into the screen. As if they know the spark will be too much. The shock too significant. I must resist.

Everything has changed since I have been here last. And yet not. I am still myself. My head is still firmly held in its place. My heart still beats in my chest. But nothing is the same.

Where did I go? I wonder again. I see glimpses. Me sitting at a coffee shop typing away about my experience. Striving to inspire.

I see her now, still. She sits beside me. Fearful of my fingers on the keys. As if she too knows the spark will be too much. The shock too significant. She may not survive.

And yet I have arrived. Grace. Fingers fluttering over the keys. I am called to write. It is no longer a story I want to share.

There is a fullness in allowing myself to Be here. Called from a deeper place. I have been longing for it. To allow myself to trust.

Is this it? I wonder. The thing I wanted to share. Not a story, but a state of Being. A depth. A possibility.

I have arrived. An imposter, finally coming home.

I wrote in a kind of rhythmic trance, without stopping, without reflecting consciously about what I was typing at all; the words arriving from a deeper, darker place, as though imposters themselves, not daring to remain in my thoughts, but merely passing through.

My arrival in late November, an imposter on my own website and in many ways my own life, had begun late on the evening of November 1, 2014. That evening, I lay in bed among the sheets atop a soft mattress laid on the floor of a spare room belonging to one of my teammates. My eyes were wide open staring at the ceiling. I was in Seattle for the second last weekend of my coaching program; it was exam weekend. We had completed one day of tests with more to follow on Sunday.

It was near midnight and I knew I should be sleeping but I could not. I was thinking about the decision I needed to make about whether to continue as a mentor coach with AC in 2015. It was an option for all graduates to continue on with the company by helping to put on the program for the next year of coaches-to-be and to get more leadership training,

Chapter 12

feedback on their coaching, and support in building a coaching practice. I had committed to do it a month earlier, but had been waffling on my decision ever since. I was also trying to decide if, in addition to continuing with AC, I wanted to renew my coaching relationship with Bay after graduating next month.

As I tried to shut off my mind's reasoning and get some sleep, energy began coursing through my body, shouting its presence and demanding I experience it. It felt related to the decisions I was trying to make, but it also felt bigger than that, and it was definitely more than just exam nerves. Slowly, I began to move toward it, ignoring my mind's orders of sleep. As I let myself sink into it I could feel something building around my heart, in whispers at first, then growing louder and expanding into a resonating truth. I reached for my iPhone, opened my Notes App, and without thinking began to type.

I don't accept the offer of advancement with AC, because I don't see my worthiness.

When I don't see my worthiness I compare myself to others.

When I compare myself to others, if I accept their invitation to step forward I lose and they win.

So I don't step forward.

It's not a competition; it's an invitation.

I am invited because others see my worthiness and they see me there with them, not because they want to win some imaginary game.

When I love myself I can see that I am worthy of the invitation.

I only have to step forward and I am free.

I have been withholding my love for powerful leadership because I've withheld acknowledging myself as a powerful leader.

I keep my heart closed to others because I've kept my heart closed to myself.

It's all about loving myself.
I love myself. It's all about loving myself.
I love myself.
I love each of my teammates. So much.
I love the experience of this program.
I love coaching.
I love being a coach.
I love being with people.
I love creating.
I love myself.
I declare that it's time to fly.
Passion.
Creation from love.
I am worthy of all the love.
It's time to let it in.

My becoming an imposter likely began even before these words were written. Perhaps it began as a seed when I got my first coaching client, sprouting when I got my second and made my first passionate speech. Perhaps it began to bud and blossom as I grew into the leadership role I had taken on among my coaching teammates in October, when I organized the volunteers for our November oral exams. Or perhaps, more likely the case, it had begun long before that, in the moment I pressed "send," thereby cancelling my 5:30 a.m. run late one evening in early January, 2013. Regardless of when I had sown the seed, my harvest was beginning to ripen.

Earlier in the year, my teammates and I had each completed an exercise to discover our life purpose. The exercise involved distilling down to one word the essence of what we were meant to be and create in this life. What I had come up with was the word "passion," which, at the time we completed the exercise, I

Chapter 12

mostly related to in a broad intellectual way to include a state of being, acting, and creating in myself, and inspiring that same passion in others. I believed that if everyone in the world were living from their own unique passion deep within, the world would be a much more beautiful, peaceful, loving, joy-filled place; anything would be possible. I knew that the times I felt most joy and peace in myself were when I was passionately engaging with someone or creating something. I knew that passion is where I feel most alive. I often wrote passionately on TYS and was engaging in more and more passionate speaking and poetry. I loved those moments. I wanted to create more of them.

I had already transformed my life circumstances enough that I was spending a good chunk of my time dreaming about my passions and then creating them. My life contained significantly more passion than ever before. And yet, something was still missing. My schedule still often filled to the point I was not enjoying anything I was up to, and although I was constantly trying to be fully committed to both my legal career and my coaching practice, I often felt one was pitted against the other: I found myself pulled in different directions. I was deep in the process of figuring out this conundrum. I knew it had something to do with a bigger purpose and with love, and sometimes I thought I had it all figured out, but I could not yet fully see the trap I had set for myself, or the way out.

That Saturday evening of exam weekend in November 2014, I chipped away the last hold on a large section of the wall I had built around my carefully crafted world and that wall came tumbling down, creating a mountain of rubble and revealing something I had been looking for within myself. Although I didn't realize the power of the words I had tapped into my iPhone or the full impact they would create in my life in the moment, I knew the declaration I made to myself to let love in had created a shift in my internal world. I could now feel that what passion meant to me was creation from love. In order to create from love, I had to let the love in. I was ready. I had just committed to my life purpose of passion at a whole new level.

Over the next few weeks, this shift radically transformed my life in ways I could not have predicted. The first shift I noticed was that even as I lay there in bed, I knew with more certainty I wanted to be a great coach and leader, and that I would continue on next year for more leadership training as a mentor coach with AC. I also knew I wanted to continue my coaching relationship with Bay.

The next day I experienced more deeply the impact of my breakthrough. After our exams were over, I declared I would be staying on as a mentor coach and made my second passionate speech to a room full of coaches–to–be, receiving a standing ovation from my teammates.

That evening on the drive home from Seattle, the impact grew. As I drove, I offered some coaching reflections to Scott, the same teammate who had offered a powerful reflection to me a few months earlier regarding my relationship to commitment. He was riding shotgun next to me, and, as we were speaking, I began to allow myself to open my heart and powerfully share what I saw for him.

Something I said got past his defenses and an energetic force field opened up. My entire body became electrified with the energy coursing between us and I felt fullness like I'd rarely felt before. For the next hour of our drive home our conversation continued in this open electricity, my arm hairs standing on end as I drove. It felt safe to be powerful, and not in a detached controlling sort of way. It felt safe to be powerful from love.

When I awoke the next morning, my heart was still beating

Chapter 12

quickly from the energetic interaction the night before. I tried to go about my day as normal, but behind the scenes my mind was hard at work trying to make sense of what had happened. By Monday evening I admitted to myself that there was something bigger going on than simply knowing I wanted to continue on with more coaching and leadership training in 2015. The breakthrough I'd generated over the weekend in Seattle had given me access to a deeper level of my own truth. I was ready to own more boldly what I wanted throughout my life, and I felt worthy and capable of going for it.

And right on the heels of that awareness, I was hit with a ton of bricks. The two things that had been constants in my life—my current romantic relationship and my legal career—were not in alignment with my purpose at this deeper level. I loved aspects of being a lawyer, and I loved the people at my law firm, but the work did not fill me like poetry or leading and coaching from power and love. And I loved Dave, and things were going well between us, but I could now see there were levels of passion and connection that I deeply desired that we did not share. I had been hiding these truths from myself. I hadn't had the courage to hear them.

These were tough pills to swallow. I thought I had figured it all out. I had been practising commitment and loving myself fully all year. I thought back to the blog post I'd written in September about how I had figured out how to make commitment work in my romantic relationship, and how I was choosing to commit in my career. Now, merely two months after declaring to the world I was committed to both my romantic relationship and my legal career, I realized I actually wasn't.

I felt like I had stabbed myself in the back. And in the heart. My internal critic ceaselessly carried on a vicious stream of insults. "You are a hypocrite. You are a liar. You are a horrible person. You are a hypocrite. You are a liar. You are a horrible person."

I had a massive breakdown. My entire body shut down. For three days I lay in bed with a mix of symptoms between a bad cold and a full-bodied flu. I was snot-filled and feverish. My skin was on fire one moment and ravaged with uncontrollable shivers the next. My organs were waterlogged and pressure-cooked. A pulsing ache found its way into every inch of my body inside and out. I could barely move. My emotions and my internal critic were on overdrive.

"You are a hypocrite. You are a liar. You are a horrible person. You are a hypocrite. You are a liar. You are a horrible person. You are a hypocrite. You are a liar. You are a horrible person."

I desperately wanted a resolution, a way forward that would give me peace from this invisible war going on inside me. I did not know what to do.

Full-bodied Love

"The Glance"
An inkling.
Timid beginning.
Dancing in waves.
An indulgence.
Playful stealth.
Overflowing the heart.
An ember.
Deep hearth.
Spreading the wild.
An appreciation.
Gentle opening.
Plunging to depths.

Chapter 12

An invitation.
Love calling.
Meeting of souls.

I had to be willing to be wrong about everything. About things I had said. Things I had written. Things I had done. I had to be willing to let go of my own expectations. I had to be willing to let my ego be pulverized. I had to be willing to disappoint others. I had to be willing to let my heart break. I had to be willing to break the hearts of others.

Perhaps the biggest risk of all I took was with my heart. As my emotionally clogged body and my internal critic slowly quieted, I began to uncover the cause of my inner turmoil. A door I had kept safely locked over my heart had broken open on that drive home from Seattle and I could hear the deeper truth whispering in my soul: "I am in love." The words sent fire spreading through my body.

"I am in love with Scott."

I was stunned that something so powerful could have come about so suddenly. Although we had been friends for nearly a year, it wasn't until that moment while we were driving that I had ever felt attraction or had a single romantic thought involving Scott. It could not be. For the next week I tried to convince myself it was not true, coming up with every rational explanation I could think of for why my entire body was alive in a way I had long forgotten possible.

"This is not romantic love. Maybe it's deep friendship. Maybe it's a soul connection. It doesn't mean I'm in love. It's probably just a coaching breakthrough. It's beautiful information about a new depth of connection that is possible for me. It's something I can create anywhere. I can create this with Dave. I am not in love with someone else. I am not in love. I am not in love!"

I rationalized this way over and over, willing myself to believe it with such force that for a few days I did. I tried to find words to communicate what was going on inside me with the man I was living with, whom I loved. I tried to have conversations about the possibility of creating a deeper more passionate soul connection between us. We had different ideas about passion. Dave thought I wanted more drama and wasn't interested in that. I tried to explain what I wanted in a way that would bring us to the same page, but, despite the fact that my heart was breaking from the pain I was causing both Dave and myself, I couldn't explain what I wanted wholeheartedly. A part of me would not believe my mind's rational way forward. My heart was already out, and although I did not want to admit it, it had never fully been in in the first place. I had loved Dave, but I had never been in *love*.

Two weeks after the full-bodied coaching experience with Scott, I could no longer ignore the fiery truth in my heart. I was in love. After getting out of the city and taking a four-day solo visioning workshop in Chicago, my mind's rational arguments no longer held any weight. Not only did I need to leave my law firm and trust fully in my ability to build my coaching practice and writing into a viable business, but I knew I needed to end my romantic relationship too.

I gave notice at my law firm and ended my relationship as soon as I returned home in mid-November.

The moment I fully committed to my new life, the Universe shifted with me. Within two weeks of giving notice at my law firm, I was hired twice by new coaching clients, and Jamie, although disappointed I would be leaving his law office, agreed to come down to Seattle to my coaching program graduation at the beginning of December. When I left my romantic relationship, I had nowhere to live. I moved out of the apartment

Chapter 12

we were sharing and into a friend's spare bedroom for the week. In the spirit of love I was engulfed in, I decided to hand over to the Universe one more aspect of my life and live nomadically for a year. I started talking to a few people about the adventure I was embarking on and simply trusted I would find a new home. Within a few days I had living arrangements lined up for the next two and a half months: some extended stays in spare bedrooms of friends, and some house-sitting and cat-sitting opportunities, all at no cost.

As I gave myself permission to accept my truth, the bliss of new love began taking over. For the last two weeks of November and the beginning of December my life was ecstasy. I was completely engrossed in the excitement of new things and head over heels in love everywhere—with Scott, my new career, my coaching clients, and my team at my coaching program. Poetry poured out of me in buckets and I made a declaration that I would write one poem every weekday for all of 2015 and publish it on my Facebook newsfeed.

I felt deeply connected to my body in a way I never had before. I was exercising and eating intuitively—hearing for the first time whispers of that body wisdom I for-so-long believed was a myth. I was feeling sexy. My entire body buzzed with energy. I was present to life all around me in the air, the ground, the sky, and the trees. I felt a link with every soul in the entire world. I practically skipped to work and down the halls at my law office. I gave extra hugs to friends and sent "I love yous" over phone lines, emails, and Facebook messenger. I said hello to people on the street, paid them a compliment, and wished them a lovely day. I wanted to wrap my arms around the entire world and say, thank you!

Like a starry-eyed character in a movie, I had arrived at my happy ending. Finally, I loved everything about my life. This was the breakthrough I was waiting for. Nothing could be more perfect.

Chapter 13—Something Greater

A Foggy Night

It was a cool, clear evening in early January. The dreary drizzle that had been lingering all day had lifted, leaving the air moist but clear. I looked up at the sky as I waited for the bus that would take me to Scott's for the night. Even the clouds had parted, revealing a sprinkling of stars somewhat dulled by the city lights.

I had been working on my client game all day at a little café in Kitsilano, one of my favourite neighbourhoods in Vancouver, sending out offers of sample coaching sessions to people I would love to work with and requests for referrals from people who might know someone who would be a good fit for coaching with me. I hadn't made much progress and I was exhausted. Every action I had taken had felt hard; like I was working through a thick fog. I had told myself it was the weather and pushed on, but even though the night sky had now cleared, I still felt groggy and ungrounded, like I was suspended in the air with my head in a cloud, my feet unable to reach solid ground.

"What is this about?" I thought.

I turned my attention inward and felt a poem begin to form. I reached for my iPhone, opened my Notes App, and began to type:

"A Foggy Night"
My shoes are worn, and yet, I cannot feel
the earth coming up

I Am Enough

to meet my soles. My feet
are swollen. Each step padded,
and numb. Staring…

"My dear, can you help me?" The voice jolted me from my writing and fiery energy began coursing up my left arm. Skin prickling, I looked at the hand that had come to rest on my left forearm, before adjusting my gaze to take in the woman to whom it belonged. She was short, at the most five feet, her rounded figure clothed in a flowing white dress that reached both to her wrists and to her toes. Feathery jewellery hung down her front and dangled from her ears. She wore no jacket, only a knee-length brown suede vest. Her face was weathered and framed with long wisps of silver hair. Plump cheeks sat on each end of her warm smile, coming up to meet the deep crinkles around her eyes. As I took in her piercing hazel stare, I was met with a startling mixture of innocence and wisdom, and a twinkle of something I couldn't quite put my finger on. Her hand again squeezed my arm, sending heat through the sleeve of my rain jacket and up my arm to my shoulder from every point of contact. My pulse quickened.

"My dear, can you help me?" she repeated.

"What do you need help with?" I asked, still engaged in the visceral impact of her presence.

"Can you tell me if the number nine stops here?" she said. "I have a migraine. I can't read the sign. Everything is covered with bright white spots."

"Yes," I said, trying to pull myself from my energetic inner world. "The nine stops here. It's the bus I need too. It should be here in a few minutes."

"Thank you, dear," she replied, sitting down on the bench next to me and removing her fingers from their grip around

Chapter 13

my arm. I could feel the energy that had been flowing into me reverse its course and leave with her touch. I felt unsettled. As I turned back to continue my poem I realized my phone was no longer in my hand; I had unconsciously slipped it into my pocket.

"I get these migraines all the time." She had turned toward me and was speaking again. "It comes with the gift."

I looked over. Her face was animated like a child's. My breath caught in my lungs as I again met her eyes. They were disarming.

She smiled and continued. "They don't last very long, but they are fierce. I felt this one coming on as I was leaving my friend's place. It's already lifting. Another moment or two it will be gone."

She stopped short; her eyes darted up and down my body and came to rest on my heart, reminding me of how a deer, hearing some distant sound in the forest, freezes and perks up its ears.

"My dear, are you okay?" she asked, her eyes filled with concern as she scanned my face. "Your aura is a thick grey fog."

My heart began racing again, as the thought of my unfinished poem and the fog I had been attempting to operate through all day flashed through my mind.

"I'm okay," I replied, feeling my defences fly up all around me.

"Do you mind if I do a reading?" she continued as if I hadn't spoken at all. "I work with energy."

"Of course," I thought. "She's an energy healer." I knew about reiki. I hadn't ever tried it, but some of my friends had, and had described the experience as helpful and healing. Her words offered me an explanation for the energetic intensity of our interaction. I relaxed. I was curious.

"Okay, sure," I said.

She began humming as she reached her palms of fire toward

me, passing them over my body from top to bottom, stopping here and there, and saying things like "Hmm" and "Tsss" before continuing on. Despite the fact that her palms never made contact with my clothing or my skin, electricity coursed through me, following their movement.

Her examination came to an end with her palms hovering over my chest. She let them linger there for a moment more before dropping them to her lap.

"You have wrapped yourself in a thick blanket of fog; like some kind of self-made confusion. Especially, here," she said, pointing at my heart. "There's a dark grey cloud here."

Emotions began stirring in my gut. I felt my defences nearby readying to take up their position around me and shut this woman out.

"A foggy grey aura represents fear. You are trying to avoid something." She continued, the twinkle never leaving her eyes, "I would take a look at that if I were you. You'll get sick if that kind of fear lingers too long."

The emotion that had been stirring gathered into a lump and dropped to the floor of my gut like a rock. On some level I knew what she was saying was true. I had been feeling like I was in a fog. And it wasn't just today. I had mostly ignored it or blamed it on the weather, but the fog had been hovering and growing in intensity for over a week. I knew my patterns well enough by now to know that I often did use confusion as a way of avoiding my fears. "Was I really creating this fog myself?" I wondered.

Just then a bus pulled up in front of us. It was the nine. Grateful for the distraction from our conversation I got up.

"This is our bus," I said.

Once on the bus I sat down and turned my face toward the window, hoping she would take the hint that I no longer wanted to continue our conversation.

Chapter 13

She sat down on the seat beside me.

"Where are you off to?" she asked.

"My boyfriend's," I answered, frustrated that she had ignored my subtle attempt to be alone, but grateful she had chosen a new topic of conversation.

"I'm from Vancouver Island," she continued, clearly in the mood for conversation. "I'm in town for a few weeks to help a friend. She's just divorced and going through a rough time. Have you ever been to the Island?"

"I've been to Victoria a few times," I replied, trying to keep my responses as short as possible.

"I'm in Nanaimo," she continued. "I love it there. I was born in Edmonton, but I've been on the Island for over forty years now. It's so beautiful. I could never go back."

I felt myself softening again, becoming more open to conversation. "I know what you mean," I said. "I'm originally from Manitoba. My family's still there, but the coast feels like home."

"I have a huge family back in Alberta," she replied. "I'm leaving from here to go visit them at the end of the month."

"That's nice," I responded. "I have a big family too. I try to go back and visit a few times a year."

"I'm looking forward to seeing my Uncle George the most," she continued. "He's almost ninety now, but he's still with it most of the time. He's had a wild life. Always has a story to tell."

As the bus made its way from stop to stop, the rush of words continued to flow from her mouth. I learned about the various members of her family and some of their stories; about her life in Nanaimo on Vancouver Island; and about her mid-life spiritual awakening and her recent work as a mystic offering psychic and tarot card readings and energy healings. In between her stories, I shared a sentence or two about some of the recent changes I had made in my life and the nomadic adventure I was embarking on this year. As we came up to her stop she took a pen and paper out of her bag and wrote "Ada" and beside it her number.

"We will meet again," she said decisively as she handed me the note, and with a wave that jingled all the bracelets on her wrist, she stepped off the bus.

I put the paper in my pocket and said goodbye as the door closed behind her. The bus pulled away and I turned my head toward the window. She was already gone.

"What did she mean, 'We will meet again'?" I thought. "It's possible, of course. But what a strange thing to say with such confidence."

The unsettled feeling returned, and once again I remembered my unfinished poem. I pulled my phone from my pocket and read what I had written:

"A Foggy Night"
My shoes are worn, and yet, I cannot feel
the earth coming up
to meet my soles. My feet
are swollen. Each step padded,
and numb. Staring…

I continued:

at the solid mass beneath my feet
I keep walking, and yet,
I am stopped.
My limbs are frozen. Flailing
to feel the moist night. The heat

Chapter 13

> *is right there, but an invisible shield*
> *blocks me from feeling warmth. My hands*
> *are reaching. Up*
> *into a fog*
> *of cellophane.*

A few minutes later I had arrived at my stop. I posted my daily poem to my Facebook feed, and put my phone back in my bag. As I stood to get off the bus I noticed something sparkling on the seat beside me. It was a beautiful rose-coloured stone. It was hers. I had seen it as she had rifled through her bag for a pen.

"I have to return it," I thought, the unsettled feeling growing inside me as I picked it up and walked off the bus. "I guess we will meet again."

Waking Up

When I woke up the next morning, the fog had lifted and the reality that I had upended my life had officially set in. As my mind does, it began trying really hard to make sense of the fear and figuring out what to do with it.

"Of course you are scared, Danielle!" My mind reeled. "Not two months ago, in the span of two weeks, you ended a serious commitment to your romantic partner, you fell head over heels in love, and you dove into a relationship with someone new. You decided to leave the career you've spent ten years preparing for and building, you committed to another year of serious personal transformation as a mentor coach with AC, and you threw yourself headfirst into a new business venture based in creativity and love. You gave up your home and you decided to be a nomad for a year. On top of all of those mountainous challenges, you declared 2015 to be a year of slowing down. You are no longer guaranteed a paycheque and you are homeless. And you expect yourself not to be scared! Are you insane? What is there to figure out? Of course you are terrified! What were you thinking?"

Other than the temporary satisfaction of justifying my fears, rationalizing didn't really help. I was still scared; terrified to the point of paralysis in fact. One of my coaching clients had completed working with me in the past two weeks, and I hadn't got a new one yet. I needed to generate another client in the next two weeks to stay in integrity with the minimum number of clients I needed to be a mentor coach. I was also in the after-honeymoon-not-knowing-where-this-is-going phase of my new relationship, and wanting to be back in the bliss. I had told Scott I felt like we were meant to be together forever and he replied that while he believed we had a soul connection, he wasn't so sure about "forever." I shoved that pain down and ignored it. I was trying to wrap up a few outstanding projects at my law office, and was having trouble focusing. I had living arrangements lined up until mid-February, but that was only a month away and coming closer every day. I had no energy to deal with any of it.

Thinking about my current state of affairs didn't really help either. I felt the foundation of my life cracking beneath me. I wanted to believe I would be okay, but my mind swirled with questions that threatened to take me over. "How would I make enough money? Where would I live? Would this new relationship work out? Would my clients all leave me? Could I trust myself to not sabotage myself?"

Since hiding my fear in a fog of confusion hadn't worked for very long, and trying to figure it out wasn't really helpful, and going backwards was not an option I was willing to consider,

Chapter 13

I was forced to do something completely different. I thought back to the little moments that had given me courage to see my truth—the ones back in November, and all through 2014, that had had me choose this path in the first place. I reminded myself of something important: trust. Not just self-trust, although that was definitely part of it, but trust in something greater.

I grew up in a mildly Catholic household. Although I was baptised and as a young child participated in other traditions of the Catholic Church, by the time I was twelve we had stopped attending religious services other than with my grandma at Christmas. As an adolescent, I would have classified my faith as a question mark. In my years at university I rarely thought about religion or faith. At times, in debates with friends, I wondered about the possibility of some unseen existence. Other times, I labelled myself an atheist. Mostly, faith and conversations about faith were just not a part of my life.

It was only in 2014 that I began to think seriously about my own faith. The theme of one of the weekends of my AC program had been spirituality, and for the first time in years, or maybe ever, I had been asked to consider my relationship to the divine. As part of our homework I read a book called *Conversations with God: An Uncommon Dialogue* by Neale Donald Walsch, and a door opened inside me I hadn't realised I'd shut. As I began allowing the possibility of the divine into my life I began feeling lighter, like I didn't have to hold it all myself. I didn't know exactly what or who I believed in, but by the time I finished the book I was surprised to find I could no longer deny the existence of something greater, and even more surprised to feel a deep longing for a relationship with something universal and unseen.

Words like "soul, trust," and "Universe," and phrases like "we are all one," which I'd sometimes scoffed at in the past, began taking on deeper meaning for me. By the fall of 2014, I was open to receiving and trusting messages from the divine, and in November, I had received a powerful unseen energetic message that had given me the courage I needed to let go and take a step into the unknown.

I reminded myself of my relationship to the Universe. I kept coming back to trust. "I trust I can do this. I trust I can have it all. I trust I can have love and adventure and freedom and a new business and slow down all at the same time. I trust I will not let new things stress me out in the same way as the old things did."

I reminded myself daily. "Just trust. Just trust. Just trust."

It worked for a while, and then I would realize I wasn't really trusting. I had simply gone back to pretending everything was fine—pretending my fear wasn't there and ignoring the scary things I needed to do to get my business off the ground, or operating on top of my fear in my business and relationship and going into performance mode.

Turning It Over

"The Chameleon"
My skin can show you all the vibrancy of the natural world.
Programming too perfect.
Darkening colours on a cool evening road. Every time an impeccable result.
I pale in the light, to your growing distrust. Misunderstood, I am the prison of my dominion.
Swaying gait, stereoscopic vision, impeccable hunter. You take no notice.
They are telling tales about how I disappear when my eyes

Chapter 13

are closed.
You fail to see the misconception.
No one knows. I can change colours in two directions
at once.
Look harder, please. I am trying to communicate.

On January 13, the daily poem I wrote was called "The Chameleon." A few days later, I had a call with one of my coaching clients in which, without my saying anything, she referred to herself as a chameleon. Two days after that I had a sample session with a potential coaching client and she complained about how she felt chameleon-like; as though she didn't know who she really was because she was different in every situation. The coincidences had stacked up pretty high by this point. Although I didn't quite know why, my poem and these experiences somehow felt related to what was going on with my fears and my struggle to stay in a place of trust. What I did know was that being chameleon-like was intimately tied to my strategies of people-pleasing and perfectionism, and I was sick of it.

People-pleasing and perfectionism have been a part of my life since as long as I can remember—from excelling at school, figure skating, piano, and swimming, to perfecting my body, to being the perfect friend, girlfriend, daughter, lawyer, and partier, to saying yes to countless projects, events, and requests I wanted to say no to, to avoid disappointing someone else. On the one hand, my approval seeking had gotten me in a lot of trouble over the years, including developing an eating disorder, an unhealthy relationship with sleep, overworking, and breaking a million promises to myself. I hated these qualities I possessed. On the other hand, I now knew that my approval-seeking survival mechanisms were a part of who I am and on some unconscious level I depended on them. They had gotten me far. Much of the success I had achieved in my schooling, my career, and my relationships, I could either attribute to my ambitious perfectionist drive or to my people-pleasing connection creator.

As I developed more and more self-awareness through 2014 and early 2015, I had begun to see how pervasive these strategies were in my life. At some point in 2014, I had come to the realization that hating my survival mechanisms and trying to exorcise them from my being was not only impossible, but also not helpful. Loving my survival mechanisms—appreciating how they had gotten me to where I was, and choosing something different when I could see the strategy was no longer working or needed—was much more productive to moving forwards.

I had also realized this was much more easily said than done. Firstly, because my survival mechanisms were deeply engrained and mostly unconscious; they were habits that had built up over years and years of practice. Secondly, because they were brilliant; they could easily trick me into thinking I was not using them, when I really was. Thirdly, when I would realize I had slipped back into an old survival strategy, it was really hard to feel loving toward the part of myself that had tricked me into showing up that way.

Toward the middle of January 2015, although I didn't know it yet, I was wrestling with my survival mechanisms at a new level. The more self-aware I became, the more I started seeing differences in the way I showed up, depending on whom I was with and where I was. I felt like I was showing up as a different person everywhere—at work, with Scott, with my law friends, with my coaching friends, with my family, with my colleagues, with my clients, at my coaching program, and in every interaction I ever had. For each person I met or situation I found myself in, I brought forward the version of myself that

Chapter 13

would be the best fit, right down to the clothes I wore or the mannerisms I adopted. Some unconscious part of myself was automatically putting feelers out, gathering information about what would be best received and then guiding me to show up that way. Like a chameleon.

I could see how this strategy (which Bay and I later named "my Conspicuous Chameleon survival mechanism") had enabled me to fit in almost anywhere—from shovelling manure in a hog barn, to sipping expensive champagne forty storeys in the air, to hanging out with marathon runners, to navigating my way with only a backpack in a foreign country, to partying all night long, to speeding down the autobahn at 200 km per hour, to living in a dangerous and impoverished area of Cape Town and volunteering at an orphanage, to writing passionate poetry at 4:00 a.m., to speaking in a courtroom in front of a judge, to lying out on a bale of hay and staring at the stars.

While I was grateful for the variety of friends I had made and the unique experiences I had had all over the world, I could also see this strategy had a dark side. It was my own perfected version of people-pleasing. I wasn't just choosing to say or do things that would please others; I was actually transforming myself to a degree that who I was being in one moment felt true even if it was totally different than who I was being an hour or two later.

And then it hit me. This is why I was afraid and confused. I didn't actually know which version of me was the truth. I didn't know what was real anymore. I felt like one big lie.

Later that day, I met Ada at a coffee shop to return her stone, which I had learned from Google was rose quartz, a stone that is known for having an energetic quality of unconditional love; a stone that opens the heart chakra.

When I arrived at the coffee shop, Ada was already there,

sitting at a table by the wall, again adorned in many strands of feathery jewellery and a long flowing dress, this time in faded aquamarine. She stood as I approached, said hello, and leaned in for a hug. I felt a strange sense of electricity and comfort as I hugged her back.

"You are different today," she said before I could pull out the stone my fingers had been fumbling for in my purse. Her penetrating hazel eyes were taking me in from my feet to my head. "Your aura is a murky dark blue, which means you have some fear about the future. But there are a few gold streaks too, which means enlightenment and divine protection. You are being guided by your highest good. I'm happy the dark grey has gone. That kind of fear can be dangerous. I was worried about you."

I felt that familiar unsettling feeling; like I'd just been disarmed. I felt myself withdraw as I tried to come up with a safe response. I didn't want to have a vulnerable conversation.

"How can you see that?" I asked.

"It's just how I am," she said. "It's more of a feeling than a seeing. I can feel colours and energies around everyone, some more clearly than others. The stronger the connection, the more likely we have a purpose together. Your energy I felt strongly connected to the moment my migraine lifted on the night we met. I've continued to feel that connection off and on throughout the week. You have been changing rapidly."

"For example," she continued, "in the last few minutes your aura has developed a neon yellow haze. You are trying to control our interaction."

For a moment, my defences intensified and I tried to withdraw internally even further. And then I felt something let go. As strange as our interactions had been so far, I did like this woman. And I did feel we had met for a reason. Fear and withdrawal were getting me nowhere. I needed to trust.

Chapter 13

"Okay," I said. "What do you think the purpose of our connection is?"

"What it's always about," she replied. "Healing. Yours and the world's. I sense you are struggling with something right now. I can help you, so you can help others. Love will spread. It's the only way to save the world."

I breathed in. It felt true. I was struggling with something. I did want to heal myself and the world, more than anything. And I knew that love was the answer. I decided to share what was going on for me. Before I could say anything, she spoke.

"Your energy is changing again." She paused. "You have shape-shifter energy. Like a chameleon."

My heart began to race at lightning speed. I held my breath.

"This is what you are struggling with, isn't it?" she said, sensing my fear. "Don't worry. It's not a bad thing. Shape-shifter energy can be painful when operating unconsciously because it controls you. But it's actually a powerful gift if you can harness it."

I felt a swirl of emotions. An image of a tree changing colours in the fall filled my mind as I tried to process what she had said. I remembered the conversation I had had with my mentor in Victoria. She had lived through many different experiences, relationships, and roles in her life, but instead of feeling like a chameleon, she had felt like a tree, grounded and trusting in a strong sense of who she is.

"This is what it means to be a tree," I thought, "to operate from a deep knowing of who I am." From that knowing I can consciously choose to change my colours and step into the role of a lawyer or a coach and a million other things, including standing more strongly in my relationships, without feeling like I am hiding or losing parts of myself. It felt like a huge weight had been lifted off my shoulders. There was nothing

I Am Enough

wrong with me. I wasn't a horrible person and a liar. I simply needed to continue on my path of getting to know myself.

Ada, who had been watching me intensely as I processed, stood up and said it was time for her to go. Her friend was waiting. I snapped myself out of my inner world, thanked her, and said I would think some more about what she had said.

"Keep it," she said, as I reached for my purse to get her stone. "I sense you will need it soon."

Chapter 14—Wild Love

The Wild Love I Thought I Knew

My phone buzzed. I looked up from the legal work I was attempting to focus on, to a text message with a flurry of heart emoticons. My pulse quickened. My stomach fluttered. My face broke into a smile as heat rose into my cheeks. I opened the message and sent a flurry of love back.

I thought back to the first time we had seen each other after that fateful November car ride. We had met at a coffee shop on the pretense of working on our individual writing projects as we had in the past, only the tension in the air made it impossible. It was like our energies had magnetized and were pulling us together. I already knew I was in love. We stopped talking around it.

"I just want to tell you I love you, over and over," Scott had said, and I melted right into my seat. Just as I had again now, two months later, sending heart shapes and kisses over the phone. I had never experienced a connection like this before: passionate, fiery chemistry, mixed with intellectual conversation, deep soulful love, play, and a feeling of home. My limbs could have spent days entwined in his without any desire to move. And that hadn't been too far from reality. Every spare moment I had had between wrapping up my legal work and coaching was spent consumed by that whole-bodied bliss; desire and longing grew quickly each time we were apart.

By this time, I knew I was a passionate woman. I knew I loved to fall in love. And I knew I loved to do everything with a touch of madness—from midnight revelations about life, to writing affidavits at 3:00 a.m., to quitting my entire life all at once. In my world, being in love means losing control, forgetting anything else exists, spending hours curled up together staring in each other's eyes, making bold life decisions in love's name. Love was the perfect excuse for me to let out my wild side. This is what I thought it meant to live my life purpose; to be madly in love with some new creation or person; to fly with reckless abandon on the coattails of love.

In the past, I had often been too scared to be outwardly expressively romantic or passionate. I had often held myself back from even feeling it. But by the end of 2014, I was starting to get a sense that love was the centre of the thing I was on a mission to understand (life) and the answer to the thing I was trying to achieve (fulfillment). This time I was not holding back. I allowed myself to be completely engulfed by love in a way I hadn't since falling in love for the first time when I was sixteen. I was distracted at work, I lost my appetite—in fact I was not thinking about food at all, which was incredible for me—and my physical body was present and alive like someone had turned on a switch.

I had thought it was everything, at least for a few weeks. But by mid-January, fears had begun sneaking back into my life, and doubts had started showing up in my relationship. Despite the fact that feelings of love still did me in in the moment, I was starting to see there was still something missing.

Love, The Philosophy

"Wholeness." My body tingled as I said it, giving me that knowing feeling I had received something true.

I had been cross-legged for about ten minutes in front of

Chapter 14

the mirror in the spare bedroom of my friend's apartment where I was cat-sitting, a lit candle beside me and a note paper showing the words, "I am sacred." I had been meditating on the mantra "I am sacred," inspired by a suggestion by Elizabeth DiAlto, the creator of Wild Soul Movement. Over the past week I had spent a lot of time alone, trying to get in touch with my true self so I could strengthen it. Following Wild Soul Movement online became a source of inspiration about how I might do that. Other sources were two books I was reading—a book Bay had recommended called *The Dark Side of the Light Chasers* by Debbie Ford and *Reveal: A Sacred Manual for Getting Spiritually Naked* by Meggan Watterson, signed by the author herself when I had attended her book launch in New York two years earlier.

"Wholeness." The word had made its way out of my mouth as if by its own determination. I felt pieces shifting inside me, as though thousands of oddly shaped parts that had been scattered around were making their way into their proper places. Something was being created. A picture was coming together.

It felt like what was arriving was larger than me; as though I wouldn't be able to hold it all at once. I was going to need to write this down. I pulled out my notepad and a pen and wrote the word "wholeness." Only five minutes earlier "wholeness" had simply been another word. Somehow it now felt like this word was everything I had been searching for.

I waited. There had to be some kind of explanation to this revelation. Five minutes. Ten minutes. Nothing came. I waited a few more minutes. I still felt like something had shifted into place, but I couldn't quite articulate it. My mind, getting frustrated with waiting, began trying to figure it out. I wrote.

I Am Enough

Wholeness. The whole journey. My journey. Trash your stress. Self-love. Passion. Purpose. Create a life you love. Being good enough = self-love = loving my human limitations = loving others. Judgment of self = judgment of others. *Reveal* = listen to the voice of your soul. *Wild Soul Movement* = get into your body = your wild soul. *Dark Side of the Light Chasers* = we are all one = we are all traits in the Universe = wholeness.

I was dancing around it but I hadn't yet got it. I sighed and let it go. I was trying to force an answer that wasn't ready. I put the notepad down and looked toward the mirror. "Just trust. It's okay." I put my hands to my heart and bowed to myself in the mirror.

"You are sacred," I whispered.

Something settled in my gut. My hand moved back to the paper and wrote, "Self-love = wholeness."

"Yes," I whispered. I sank into my seat and let the truth sink in. "I possess the possibility of every human characteristic. True self-love is allowing that wholeness to be okay."

This was the first of many aha moments I experienced over the next week as my budding philosophy came to life. The fear and the fog that had settled over my life for the past month began to lift and fresh scents of love and possibility arrived in my world.

Within the next few days I got hired by a new client; copy for my new website started flowing out of me; I began working on a course to offer to my coaching clients based on my new philosophy; I wrapped up a project I had been struggling to complete at my law office; I had a major breakthrough in the leadership role I had taken on as a mentor coach; Scott and I grew closer and he decided to join me on my nomadic adventure; and an offer of a new home arrived giving us a place to live until sometime in March.

Chapter 14

About a week later as I was running over to Scott's place to help him pack up his things, I was excited, inspired, and ready to embrace all of this next stage of my life, fear and chameleon survival mechanism included. Part way over the Cambie Street Bridge, feet flying underneath me, an intense feeling of joy began spreading throughout my body, and I stopped to capture these words as they flew out of my soul.

> ***"Remembered"***
> *"I can speak to it," she called. Hand waving in the air.*
> *I know it. I know the answer.*
> *All of it.*
> *Every question, every answer. Every decision. Every indecision.*
> *All of the indecision.*
> *"I can speak to it," she cried.*
> *Every conversation. Every experience. Every hand held too long in suffering.*
> *All of the suffering.*
> *"I can speak to it," she sobbed.*
> *Every gaze. Every spark. Every thing lighted on fire and forgotten.*
> *All of the forgotten.*
> *I have remembered.*

By mid-February 2015, I had completed all the lingering projects at my law office, and I was focusing on coaching and my other creative pursuits full time. I was feeling solid in my philosophy that formed the foundation for my work, two of my four current coaching clients signed up for a twelve-month pilot of the course I was creating called "Remembering Wholeness: The Ultimate Gift," based on my philosophy, and my new website was almost ready to launch.

A little over a week later, although I didn't feel like I had it all figured out perfectly yet, I launched my new website, www.DanielleRondeau.com, read over my new philosophy one last time, and uploaded it into the world.

About My Work

Five beliefs underlie my work:

1. Personal development is a journey of self-love.
2. Self-love is wholeness.
3. Wholeness is oneness.
4. Oneness is freedom.
5. All there is for us to do is to remember.

In our individualistic culture we are resigned to disconnection. So intense is the pain of disconnection, that we create a multitude of ways to avoid it. From addictions to violence to busyness to mindless entertainment, our society is filled with the side effects of avoiding feeling the pain of disconnection.

At the root of our culture's pain is a disconnection from ourselves. We have forgotten who we are. We have denied and repressed so many aspects of ourselves that the image we show the world and even the one we show ourselves is always fragmented. We become exhausted trying to live only in acceptable parts of who we are.

Personal development is at its core, self-love. The explosion of personal development is our culture's answer to the realization that we have forgotten who we are and how to be ourselves. The personal-development journey of healing and shifting the beliefs that limit our possibilities, how we show up, and who we allow ourselves to be create the journey of rediscovery of self and self-love.

Complete self-love is wholeness. Self-love as an action is the act of re-welcoming the repressed or denied aspects of who we are and removing self-imposed limits on our being. Self-love as a state of being is wholeness, having full access to the limitless ways of being that we possessed when we came into this world.

Self-love or wholeness is also oneness. The ways we create disconnection and the judgments we have about others mirror the parts of ourselves we have denied or refused to love. When we remove the self-imposed limits on our connection with ourselves, we also remove the limits on our connection with others. When we are whole we are one.

We desire oneness because it is freedom. As one, we no longer live our lives trying to avoid the pain of disconnection. We no longer live in fear of loss, rejection, or abandonment. From a state of being already connected and wholly loved, there is nowhere to get to, and therefore, we are free to go wherever we please. All expressions, experiences, and life paths are open.

Wholeness and oneness are not destinations. We do not need to do anything or be any different in order to get to them. All we must be is willing to remember, with love, all of who we already are.

It is time to remember.

A Love that is Wilder Still

For the last few days of February and the first week of March, Scott and I stayed with his parents on their farm on Vancouver Island. It is a beautiful, peaceful setting, which was perfect for me as I was in a bit of a frenzy trying to get the details of my new coaching course ready for launch. I had also taken on a leadership role on a project for the next AC weekend. Everything had to be ready to go by the first weekend in March, and the project was currently in breakdown. Scott had not continued on with AC as a mentor coach, but he knew that I was overwhelmed with AC and everything else, and he was being incredibly supportive. He was helping me work through the issues I was having (including talking me off a ledge of simply quitting my role as a mentor coach), bringing me snacks, and requiring me to take much-needed breaks from coaching, planning, and course building. We enjoyed long walks by the water, delicious meals with his parents, and a date night out in the nearby town.

By the time Friday rolled around, most things had fallen into place. I had successfully launched my course and sent out the first week's materials to my clients, and my mentor coach team had generated the breakthrough we needed. Our project was ready for the weekend. In every ounce of my being I felt gratitude. Gratitude for the team of people I worked with and who supported me at AC, gratitude for my clients, gratitude for the beautiful setting we had been living in all week, and most of all, gratitude for Scott who had been so loving and supportive when I needed it most. I left him a card hidden among his things expressing my appreciation and headed down to Seattle for a weekend of transformation, love, and being.

Returning from Seattle two days later, I found that my world had flipped on its head: Scott didn't want to see me. He said he felt like he had gone into caretaking mode last week and didn't like how we were interacting. He felt resistance to even talking to me on the phone. I didn't understand. I thought everything had been going so well. It felt like I'd been stabbed in the gut. What I thought had been support from a place of love hadn't been. After a brief moment of anger toward him I turned the blame inwards on myself. "Why was I leaning on him so much? Why was I so needy? Why couldn't I love myself more? Why wasn't I stronger? Why didn't I show up more powerfully in our relationship?"

It was too painful to think about. I made myself wrong for all of it and closed my heart to the pain hoping it would magically work itself out.

Two days later as I was out getting some groceries near the friend's place where I was staying in Vancouver, the Universe tried to jolt me out of my numbed-out state with a powerful experience of my own philosophy. As I paused at a traffic light, my whole body was overcome with an exquisite blissful feeling: love. It woke me up for a moment and I captured the experience in a poem.

"Wild Love"

I thought I knew wild love.
Whispers of sweet love tumbling bodies and kisses down meadowed hills and clothes-strewn beaches at dusk.
I have had those times.
They were glorious and there was love there, and I spent so much time trying to get there when I was not.
A part of me was still not free.
Today I was by myself walking the sidewalk of a busy street and it occurred to me to allow myself my experience.
I allowed myself my experience.
The tyranny of words around my world for a moment lifted and I was one with the city street air.
Liberated I kept walking.
I thought this is how the peonies must feel as they bloom lusciously in midday.
Radiant and unbridled.
A simple practice of saying yes to myself.
This is how wild love is meant to go.
No wilder love there is.

I felt intense peace and love. Everything was okay as it was. I was okay. I tried to stay there as I went about my grocery shopping, but the feeling slipped away, and my reality was all still too painful to be with. By the time I returned home, I had again locked up my heart. The next morning, I filled my schedule for the rest of the week so full I would not have time to breathe, never mind feel.

By Friday I had run out of steam on my list of distractions and was resorting to old habits of emotional eating to avoid my pain. Late Friday morning as I sat at the kitchen table of a different friend I was now staying with eating steadily even though I was not hungry, and even though I was fully aware that the only reason I was eating was to avoid feeling my feelings, I stopped for a moment mid-mouthful and decided it was time to face this. I called deep on my courage and breathed my awareness back into my body. What had been a dull ache in my chest became a searing pain in my heart. Tears began flowing.

The pain was huge. I didn't want to be alone with it. I called deep on my courage again, picked up the phone, and called Steph, one of my closest friends, and the only other member of last year's Van City Coach Crew who had decided to stay on as a mentor coach. After our call and a long emotional bath, I decided to reach out for a little more support from teammates on our private mentor coach blog.

I sat down and wrote to my team about the pain I was experiencing and how I had been avoiding it all week with various coping mechanisms. I shared what was going on in my relationship, including how heartbroken I was feeling, and how frustrated I was that I didn't know what to do differently. I had been typing my blog post for a few moments when I began realizing a deeper truth. I stopped and let it sink in. I kept writing.

Chapter 14

What I'm heartbroken about is not only my relationship with Scott. I love that guy so much my heart feels like it will explode with pain every time I think about him. And I can see that what I am really heartbroken about is all the times I have closed my own heart to love. What I am standing for now is love. Living like this. With my heart wide open. Not making myself wrong for feeling. Not pushing my emotions down or holding them as inconvenient or in the way of doing my client game or other things I want in life.

This is what I want. Living fully. This is what I have been fighting for this entire journey. Allowing love to be so powerful that nothing else matters. In this moment I can feel it. The love in my heart is so powerful it terrifies me and a part of me wants to eat some more to numb it. But actually I don't. I want to feel it. This is the place of creation, from love. This is what I want for the world. Nothing else is real.

My teary breakdown led to a breakthrough in power. And what that looked like was not how I was trying to make it look at all (making myself busy and pushing through). It simply looked like love. The next day, Scott and I had a heartfelt conversation on the phone about our experience over the past week and expressed what we needed from each other and our relationship. From that new level of openness and vulnerability we arrived at a deeper connection with each other, and renewed desire and love. I could feel I was being different with him in our conversation—not attached—simply committed to love.

We met up at the spare apartment of my mentor in Victoria over the weekend, the next planned stop on our nomadic adventure, and continued our relationship with a new depth of honesty and love.

My client game also shifted. On Friday afternoon after my cry I had a powerful enrollment conversation with a potential client. On Monday, I had two more. On Wednesday, I was hired by a young lawyer looking to reduce her anxiety, discover her passions, stop people-pleasing, and learn to love herself and her life more fully. I was no longer stopping where I usually stopped in my enrollment of new clients. I no longer felt like I was pressuring or trying to convince these new clients. I wasn't attached to getting hired. I simply felt love; like I was truly standing for someone else's greatness and a more beautiful world. Nothing else mattered.

A cloud had lifted from both my romantic relationship and my business. It all felt so easy, like I had finally figured out how to play on that tricky edge of committed non-attachment. I felt peaceful and grateful. I was living my philosophy. I was allowing all of the messiness and opening doors to love.

Chapter 15— Bring on the Dark Side

Tending to the Wounds of My Inner Child

My dad, my younger brother, and I were walking through the dimly-lit halls of an old cement building. We were on our way to meet someone important: a wise old man. He was going to give my dad some secret information. I didn't know what it was about, but I had a sense that it was big and vital: something that would change the world.

We had been walking for quite some time and my brother was getting bored and tired. I was fifteen, my brother seven. He was tracing his hand along the cracks in the walls and making echoing noises down the winding halls. He wanted to go back and play in the wide open yard we had crossed to get to the front door of the building. My dad stopped walking suddenly. He looked over his shoulder at us and told me to take my brother outside to play and to wait for him to return. I was devastated. I desperately wanted to know what the old man would say. I wanted to be in on the secret. There was no discussing it. My dad insisted we go. I made a face and stomped my feet as we turned around and walked back toward the door.

Once outside, my brother laughed and ran into the field. I called for him to come back but he wasn't listening. As he neared the edge of where the open grass met the trees, he suddenly stopped and stared down toward the earth like he was looking into something. I began jogging toward him, asking what he was doing and calling for him to return. He didn't reply. As I got closer I could see he was looking into a deep hole. I shouted for him to get away from there and I picked up my pace. Just as I came within reach of him, he leaned forward and jumped in. I gasped and quickly took the last few steps to the edge of what appeared to be an old well and looked in. About fifteen feet down was my brother sitting and smiling, apparently unharmed, in a pile of what appeared to be Styrofoam.

"Are you okay? What did you jump in there for?" I screamed. "How are you ever going to get out?"

"I don't know," was all he replied, the smile never leaving his face.

"Okay," I said. "I'm going to go back inside and get Dad and a rope or something to get you out of there."

I ran back toward the building. Suddenly everything became blurry and many different scenes raced around me. As I regained my sense of awareness I realized I was with my dad listening to the old man. I was leaning against the wall, starry-eyed, completely absorbed in what he was saying. After a few minutes the old man finished talking and walked away. My dad turned to me and said he was going to the bathroom and then we would go.

As I waited I stared at the cracks in the wall. Suddenly an image of my brother at the bottom of the well flooded my mind and I realized I had forgotten what I had come inside to do. I didn't know how much time had passed but it felt like a lot. I began to panic and bolted in search of something to get him out. I ran into the old man and told him what had happened and that I needed something to get my little brother out of the well with. The old man went in search of a rope.

As he left I noticed I was holding a box in my hand. I began to cry. I knew the box contained the tools I needed to save my brother. I had been carrying it the entire time. I ran at top speed for the door, and across the yard toward the well, uneasiness swirling in my gut. As I ran I could see there was something sticking up out of the well. It looked like the leg of an animal, possibly a deer. My eyes widened in terror as I neared. The well was no longer empty. It had filled with murky brown water and there were animal carcasses floating near the top. A horrified scream escaped from my mouth.

Chapter 15

The old man arrived as if out of nowhere beside me. "Is your brother in there?" he asked calmly.

"Yes! I'm going to get him!" I replied, although a sinking feeling in my heart told me he was already dead. I got up on the edge of the well and dove in.

As my face hit the murky water, a deep haunting voice began echoing in my ears. "People are dying because you are self-absorbed."

I woke up in a cold sweat with what felt like a knife in my stomach. My entire body began to shake violently, the chilling voice still repeating in my ears. "People are dying because you are self-absorbed."

I began to cry as I reached for my phone on the night table beside me. The screen lit up: 5:46 a.m., March 20, 2015. I immediately scrolled my contacts and called my little brother in Manitoba.

"Hello?"

"Hi? Are you okay?" My voice was shaky and full of emotion.

"Yes ... what's up? Are *you* okay?"

"I had a dream ..."

Fifteen minutes later, fully reassured that my brother was okay and having profusely told him how much I loved him, my heart was still racing but I could breathe a little more easily.

This was no ordinary dream, I knew. The message I'd received at the end was like nothing I'd experienced before. It had filled me with energy, and resonated through my entire body like truth. I hadn't remembered any of my dreams since I was a young child, and even then waking memories of my dreams had been rare. So this was even more strange.

The week before, I had been feeling a little down. I hadn't gotten into an exercise routine since moving to Victoria a couple of weeks earlier; I was emotionally eating off and on; and some of my body-image frustrations were coming up. I had talked it through with Bay on our coaching call. What I realized was, even though I had discovered a new way of love from wholeness, I kept reverting back to selfish love—trying to get love and fill the void from the outside—instead of trusting I was already loved and being in relationship with others and the world from a place of being full.

I had a sense that this dream was the Universe's powerful wake-up call and invitation to do the healing work I needed to truly transform the way I love and the way I fill the void, since the message at the end of the dream was so blunt, but another part of me didn't really know what to think. I was still in shock. I loved my little brother more than anything in the world.

As I put down the phone I noticed I had missed a call while I was on the phone with my brother. My phone had been on silent so I hadn't heard it ring. My heart again began racing. Who would call me at six in the morning? It was Ada. She had left a message.

"My dear," Ada's concerned voice filled my ear, "I just woke up with a pain in my gut and a sense that it was yours and not mine. I can feel your aura. It is dark, almost black, indicating a consumption of light and a long-term lack of forgiveness. This is serious. Trust whatever energy you have received. Don't be afraid. It is here to heal you. I am sending you love. Call me if you need any support."

I sat frozen with my phone to my ear, a prickling sensation crawling up my spine. "Where was she? Could she see me? How did she know?" This was all so overwhelming. After getting over the shock that this woman was somehow deeply connected to me on an energetic level, I picked up the phone and called her back. I *had* decided to trust she was in my life to support me, I thought. Right now was not a good time to stop; I needed someone to talk me through this.

Chapter 15

After an hour on the phone with Ada, I was completely drained. She had helped me shift to a certain degree the dark veil of fear that had been wrapped around me and I had let go some of the heavy emotion. I felt a little lighter and I had access to a deeper knowing of my own truth: my original interpretation of the dream had been right. On the one hand, I was reassured the dream had nothing to do with my little brother. On the other hand, I was heartbroken. I was still unconsciously seeking approval and trying to fill the void from the outside in. The dream and the energetic message I had received at the end of the dream were the Universe's powerful ways of showing me that I was still on some level relating to everyone and everything in my life—Scott, my business, my family, my teammates, my clients, my friends, my desire to help people and save the world—from a place that was on some level selfish.

I began to cry again as I put down my phone for the second time. My body was shivering although I had no reason to be cold. I hated the thought that I was being selfish. I hated the thought that I was constantly trying to get something from relationships and from helping people. It felt manipulative. I hated the words "selfish" and "manipulative." I had always tried so hard not to be those two exact things. And yet the dream resonated as true. Part of me was coming from love, but it wasn't unconditional, universal love. I hadn't healed my own wounds and learned to love myself fully, so of course there was an element of selfishly seeking to fill my own void in my interactions with the world and with others. Teeth chattering, tears continuing to fall silently, I curled up into a ball in my bed, and fell into a deep exhausted sleep.

A few days later I was still frustrated. I very much wanted to be able to come from pure love. I wanted to be Ghandi. I wanted to be Mother Teresa. I wanted to be Jesus. Although I had only become consciously aware a little over two months ago of my default way of relating to love and the world—a way that I had developed since childhood—I was angry at myself for not being able to change it. I did recognize the impossibly high standard I had set for myself and the need to forgive myself, and so, that is the coaching request I brought to Bay a few days later.

I shared my dream with Bay and the message I had received, and we looked back into my childhood to get a clearer picture of where this strategy to get love had come from. She asked me what my childhood event was—the one my teammates and I had each shared with the group the year before during an exercise in my AC program—where I had learned the world was not safe.

"It was when my sister was born," I replied. "I was three. Up until that point I had been receiving all my parents' love and affection. I think my parents' love for me must have been very intense, as they had been devastated by the loss of their first child two years before I arrived; they had been overjoyed to have me. I must have been surrounded by so much love those first three years of my life that when my sister arrived, I began to feel rejected as some of my parents' love was diverted to her. I think my three-year-old self interpreted the whole thing to mean that love was conditional, that my sister was better than me, and that I was not good enough. I think this is why I have been comparing myself to my sister—and then other powerful women—my entire life. It probably also explains why I am operating in a power dynamic with Scott, and probably other relationships in my life. I have been trying to prove that I am worthy of the love I felt I'd lost."

Where we got to by the end of the conversation was a place

of ongoing forgiveness. We built a loving relationship with my inner child; it was actually this little girl I had left outside and forgotten, not my little brother. I needed to lovingly accept her and welcome her back into my life. I began offering love to my inner child throughout the day, especially when I was feeling rejected, needy, or broken and wanting to fill the void with external validation in the form of physical love or food. I also took on a new practice of lighting a candle each morning and sitting with a few sacred rocks and other pieces of driftwood and shells I had collected before checking in with my little one.

"It's okay to be you," I reminded her. "It's okay to be afraid. It's okay to be you, just as you are."

Forgiveness for a New Way

"Aaaargh!" My limbs flailed, my fists pounded the pillows as torrents of rage coursed through my entire body. "I haaaaate you! Aaaaargh!" Two fists at a time came down over and over and over until sweat trickled from my forehead and dripped off my nose. "It's not fair! I hate you! I hate you! I hate you!"

Scott, who had been in the other room, had already checked in to see if I was okay, and had now gone out for a walk, allowing me to complete my release. Bolting straight up off the bed my feet landed hard, pounding the floor over and over one at a time and then both launching themselves up into the air and hitting the floor in a repetitive angry thud, again and again; lungs wailing, arms waving up and down in unison with my landing, every rage-filled motion deeply satisfying on some level I did not completely understand. I indulged in the fiery energy that was coursing through me until my entire body was so exhausted I collapsed on the floor in a sweaty sobbing heap.

This was definitely the most embodied form of a completion

exercise I had taken on yet. And the most satisfying. Allowing myself to really let go and feel all of my anger was inspired partly by a little boy I had seen a few days earlier walking down the sidewalk holding his mother's hand and wailing at the top of his lungs. "Soon he will deny himself this freedom of expression," I had thought. "Soon he will deny himself this."

Since I was learning to allow myself to experience all my human qualities, and more recently had rekindled a relationship with my inner child, I was giving myself more freedom to express what I was feeling than I previously would have. The result was magical. By the time I was done feeling my feelings (and showering off the tears and sweat), I was ready to take responsibility for how my projects (and my life) had been going, and to see the gifts I had been given along the way. I ended the evening with a ceremony in which I ripped up each one of the pages of notes I'd taken throughout the day into tiny little pieces and burned them over a candle repeating the mantra: "Awareness, Acceptance, Forgiveness, Love."

It was beautiful and powerful. After I had finished burning my notes I again fell into a deep sleep. When I woke up the next morning I felt excited to start afresh; excited to create a vision to match the new way of being I was bringing into the world, one based on wholeness and self-love. The next day was April 10, 2015, and I spent the entirety of it visioning my life from a deeper connection with myself, from my vision of wholeness and oneness for the world. This is what I came up with.

Overall Life Vision

I lead everywhere in my life from love. I have the capacity to be with my whole self, and others in all states of being. I hold myself and

Chapter 15

others with love and grace. I hold space for others and stand for their greatness with ease. I am responsible for myself, my thoughts, my words, and my actions. I acknowledge, accept, forgive, and love my humanness and the humanness of others. My leadership is gentle and powerful and grounded in love and compassion. I speak my truth from the deepest core of my being. I allow my intuition to guide me in my life everywhere. I gift deep trust to myself, others, and the Divine. All parts of who I am are integrated into a beautiful whole that represents an expression of my true self. I am continually moving toward higher levels of integrity with my true self. I walk with ease and groundedness in who I am. Each part of my life is an expression of my love. I am my life and my life is me. We are one.

Self—Leadership Vision

AC supports and grounds me in my leadership, calling me forward to my vision of being in integrity with my true self in all aspects of my life. I am consistently developing deeper relationships with the team I am a part of, with the participants we are leading, and the work we are bringing into the world. I contribute my ideas, my love, and my brilliance to AC. I have helped to bring AC to Canada and to create a vibrant AC community presence in each of the program cities. My leadership comes from deep love and commitment to powerful transformation and bringing outstanding coaching and leadership into the world.

Partnership Vision

Scott and I fall more in love every day. Both of us continually access deeper love and connection and experience higher levels of growth. We call each other forward and support each other to be our greatest selves in every aspect of our lives. We appreciate and relate to each other from love and compassion. We face the world as a team. We play and laugh often and flow in life together with ease. We are consistently stepping forward into new depths of intimacy—emotional, intellectual, physical, and spiritual. We allow each other to be the one for us. We are excited to create a family together. We partner together everywhere without trying, like falling into step beside your best friend. We hold ourselves and each other as whole, complete, and perfect. We are responsible for our own thoughts, words, and actions. We are both committed to life partnership and have a strong bond that can withstand the storms of life. We have deep admiration and a passionate desire for each other. We create romance and adventure and exploration and surprise at every turn. We are at home with each other. We are one in love.

Career Vision—Wholeness Institute

I work in a castle on the water on Vancouver Island—it holds love and beauty and mystery and magic. It represents wholeness and oneness; a bringing together of Life in all its forms. The castle houses my life's work; it is a Wholeness Institute that welcomes all teachings and remembrances of who we are. My mission is to empower individuals to remember all of who they are so that they can be one again with all Life and rediscover and embrace their true selves and live in the creative freedom of that knowing.

There are many brilliant teachers and hundreds of gifted students who attend every year. The castle holds and supports us singly as individuals and together with each other and with Life. The castle is surrounded by nature. It overlooks the sea and is backed by woods with beautiful trails. Its presence represents the human soul force that lives as one with the natural world, withstanding every storm. It is the place to come to to find that force in oneself so that a person can weather her own life's storms and be in deeper connection with all Life. It is a place of self-discovery, wholeness, oneness, and freedom. It is an expression of all of who we are, of the love in our souls, and all of the ways we co-create together.

The institute houses all kinds of practices—teaching, healing, coaching, exploring, experiencing, and creating. I have eight individual clients signed up for yearlong personalized transformational programs incorporating ontological coaching, teaching, and healing. I host writing retreats, poetry readings and workshops, wholeness circles, group coaching, and classes teaching principles of wholeness. I collaborate with other professionals to bring in an embodied element including energy healing, yoga, and meditation. We host gatherings of healers and teachers and coaches and leaders of all kinds. We participate in large-scale philosophical discussions and together we collaborate on projects for cultural change.

Family Vision

My partner and I approach having children and building a family as one of the greatest adventures we can embark on as human beings. We see our children as gifts, as expressions of unconditional love, and as the chance to experience life again without limitations. We set an example for our children of what it means to live a great life in integrity with our true selves. We create a safe environment for children to grown up in, including physical, psychological, emotional, financial, and intellectual safety. Our lives are filled with love and play and a renewed sense of wonder. Our children are curious, loving, happy, healthy, courageous, and surrounded by endless love. Our home is an expression of love. It is open, by the ocean, with forest pathways nearby, a fire pit and a garden out back, sand in the front, beautiful flowers, trees, rushing water, sensual smells and lighting, warmth, comfort, play, and love. It is rustic and free. We have created an environment of nature, beauty, tranquility, sensuality, and love.

We go on trips often as a family to explore the world. We get out into nature daily. We appreciate art, music and dance, and sharing time with each other.

Community

Our family home and the Wholeness Institute are vibrant community hubs. We host weekly writing meetups, wholeness circles, and dinner gatherings. Our home is filled with dancing, singing, and deep conversation. People drop by all the time. We facilitate a community of sharing, bartering, and gifting where there is endless love. We have a few close friends and a family with whom we have deep rich loving connections. We visit and speak with them regularly. We are always meeting new people. Our circles keep expanding and growing with love.

By the time I broke my big picture vision down into smaller projects, with milestones and actions, I started feeling like this could really be my life. I was so excited. For the first time it felt like my projects were not merely projects but expressions of how I wanted to be living my life every day. Feeling a mixture of fear and excitement as I always do when I create a new vision and begin to breathe some life into it, I pushed send and shared it with my coach, and then my AC mentor coach team.

Shadow Work

Ordinary grass.
　I don't want to sit by you. I don't even see you.
　Most days I trample all over you with my fancy shoes.
　I don't know you. I don't particularly like you or dislike you. I don't know you are there.

Chapter 15

Your presence is insignificant. I could do without it, or with it. You don't matter.

Does anyone care about you? Probably not.

I cut you with a machine so big you might get lost in it, or missed, or squashed. Either way, it doesn't matter. I won't come back for you. No one will.

Maybe I will get you cut just right in the next round. Maybe not. Who cares?

You are replaceable. Boring. You could live or die. I wouldn't mind. I wouldn't likely even notice. No one would.

How do you do it? How do you keep growing? Why go on when no one cares?

Where do you find the strength to be ordinary?

Why keep feeding us who are indifferent to your existence?

You are pure love. Generosity. Selfless.

You let us bend you and squash you down and cut you and pull you out.

You continue growing year after year without acknowledgment, respect, or recognition.

I'm so scared of becoming you. Yet I've never felt so welcome.

Thank you.

I looked up from my notes. The assignment had been to sit with something that either repulses you, or that you are smitten with and introduce yourself. My introduction started out as a disgusted tirade and ended in deep admiration. I sat there in the grass, having gotten out all my fears of being ordinary, feeling deeply connected to the tiny green shoots all around me. Hyperaware that I was sitting on something alive, I suddenly felt both embarrassed and grateful, like I'd just realized my host had welcomed me in and I had walked all over the house with my dirty boots without caring.

It was Saturday, May 9, 2015, and Scott and I were at a full-day shadow work course, which involved taking a look at the character traits, or ways of being we had disowned and reintegrating them; putting wholeness into practice. It was Scott's idea to sign up, and of course, I was on board. This was right up my alley.

We went through a number of exercises throughout the day to bring our awareness to the different aspects of ourselves we did not want to see. What kept coming up for me were ordinariness and specialness. I had trouble owning aspects of both, and didn't really know how to embody either trait in what I considered a healthy way.

I thought back to the previous month when, on an inspirational high, I had messaged two of my role models in the personal development world to offer *them* coaching sessions. I had decided that I should offer to coach them after receiving a few messages via dreams and connecting with my empathic spiritual side, in a brief moment of what I called insanity. When I allow myself to recognize I am special, I often slip into arrogance. On the other hand, when I admit I am ordinary, I often slip into being broken or not good enough, and find myself looking for others to save me.

The experience I'd just had of being one with the grass was a new way of being ordinary for me. It struck a resonating cord. When I returned to the workshop after lunch I could feel something building in the same way it had when the puzzle pieces began to fall into place on my philosophy of love. I put my pen to my notebook and wrote.

The gift in ordinariness is connection.
　The pain of specialness is separation.
　The paradox of trying to receive connection is disconnection.

Chapter 15

Trying to connect = disconnect.

By trying to be a certain way in order to connect, I disconnect.

I must hold the polarities of connection and disconnection, separateness and oneness, specialness and ordinariness.

Ordinary specialness. Embrace this.

The next day I woke up to the message with more clarity. I sat down with a coffee and my journal and wrote:

The effort we make to do things gets in the way of the things themselves. The effort is a buffer, a filler. Trying creates separateness. "I will try to connect with you more" indicates there is something required to bring us together. As if we are separate and must be joined by something. From that place there can be no true connection, because the efforts and actions it takes to connect will always be between us, keeping us apart.

Yesterday I sat down in a patch of ordinary grass and felt connection resonate through me. There was nothing to do. No trying to connect. No action I took to be connected. I simply allowed myself to be present to what already is.

There's an ordinariness that must be allowed in order to experience true connection, the kind that resonates and fills the deepest hole of longing and emptiness within us. We must let go of our need to be special; different. By creating difference, we create the void, the insatiable void. I must simply allow my heart to open wide enough to remember it is already full, and fully connected to life all around me. By embracing our ordinariness, our sameness, our innate connection to all life, a different specialness emerges. Our soul, our true self, the light within us can shine freely—not in competition with others, but in connection with all life.

What I also woke up to was the reality that the issues Scott and I had come up against the previous month had not gone away. After spending the day before together at the workshop, Scott was feeling resistant toward me again. He was anxious and felt like the anxiety had something to do with the way we related to each other. He said it felt like I was attached to our relationship again and that I was not being powerful in our interactions. If I were being honest with myself, I was feeling disempowered in our relationship but I didn't know what else to do to show up differently. I was also angry that he was continually closing his heart. His persistent pulling away did not help me feel or be powerful.

We had an honest conversation and got to the heart of the issue. I wanted him to commit and build a future with me; he still wasn't sure. I shared my vision with him about what I wanted in a relationship. He said he loved my vision and he loved me but he couldn't commit. We cried a lot and in the end he decided to leave and go and stay at his parents' farm for a while. Although I was heartbroken, a part of me was peaceful. I knew this was in service of what I wanted in the long term. I also knew that by standing for what I wanted in this way, I was speaking from a place of being full; powerfully coming from my new relationship with love.

When I woke up the next morning although I was sad, I felt strong. I also felt in touch with my creative side in a way I hadn't in a while. I wanted to create. I wanted to share. I wanted to be seen. I decided to put my new wholeness muscles into practice in a creative way. On May 12, 2015, I embarked on a public wholeness challenge: a ten-day challenge in which I posted on my YouTube channel a video of myself showcasing some aspect of being human I had previously hidden or repressed. The challenge was both scary and fun, and included my eating an entire tub of ice cream on camera.

Chapter 15

Two weeks later, feeling like I had disconnected into my own little world of inner healing and wholeness, I decided to reach out and share what had been going on for me the past month with my AC team.

Hey team,
I have been doing a lot of internal work the past month, healing my childhood not-good-enough stuff and creating a powerful partnership with my little self. It's been really cool. I have this new spaciousness and the knowing that I'm going to be okay even if people reject me or my ideas. I've intellectually known that for a while, but I can really feel it in my bones now. I trust myself to take care of myself. This is huge.

Standing for what I want in my relationship with Scott and his leaving a few weeks ago was the start of my cracking open and bringing that breakthrough into the world. It's been incredible. I've shared with him powerfully what I want and I don't feel attached to him being the one I create it with. It has created access to something new for him too. I don't know what will be created between us going forward but either we will envision and commit to it together, or I will find what I'm looking for with someone else.

The thing I have been struggling with is how to crack right open and bring this breakthrough into other areas of my life. I can see it seeping in, in the deeper partnerships that I am creating through my coaching calls with my clients, and in my conversations with people here and there, but I have been nearly stopped in my client game. I don't feel scared of getting nos anymore, yet I know I am still not doing what it takes to generate a client. I could not figure out what the resistance was.

Today on my call with Bay, I realized that the fear I have not been looking at is on the other side. I'm afraid of the yesses. I'm afraid that people actually will love my vision for the world if I share it with them and then I'll have something to prove. And not only that, but they might take it from me, make it their own, and then leave me in the dust on the side of the road. I can see how this relates once again to my relationship with my sister and my parents that started when I was really little—my sister saw everything I did, started doing it herself, then did it better. I felt I was left in the dust; as though she took away my specialness.

So in service of this awareness, and moving forward powerfully in my business, I am taking on a completion exercise around my relationship to my sister and my parents from childhood on. Today. Right now.

I will be back with an update.

Love you all,

Danielle

After sending my message to my team I sat down to do a completion exercise around my childhood wounds. I felt ready.

"It really is time to forgive and let this old pain go," I thought to myself as I dove in.

My completion ended up being about the loss of my essence, the life force in my core, as my default way of being. I felt anger and grief around the creation of my survival mechanisms and the polar identities of brokenness and perfection that had become my strategies to get love. I felt some anger toward my parents and my sister, but mostly the anger was directed at myself. I allowed myself to experience the deep feelings of grief and fears of unworthiness I had been holding onto in a corner of my heart since I was a little girl. It felt so incredible to let that pain go.

When I finished feeling my feelings, I took responsibility for how I had created my own survival mechanisms as a strategy to get love. I thanked my strategies for keeping me safe and

Chapter 15

for giving me a way to "get" love all these years since I had lost touch with the truth that I always am loved. By the time I finished, I felt connected to a sense of play that I hadn't been able to access in a really long time. I felt lighter. My whole body was filled with a feeling of "of course." A feeling of knowing who I am. Knowing that I don't need to try to be inspiration or love; I just am inspiration and love.

That evening Scott and I talked on the phone. He told me he had made a decision to commit and was ready to envision how our relationship could look from both of us being committed. We talked for a while. He shared some of his process and the realizations he'd come to and I shared the new sense of power and groundedness I'd gained access to from my latest completion and the partnership I was developing with my inner child. We missed each other. We decided to try again.

After we got off the phone, I was excited and overcome with love. I sat silently staring into the space behind my closed eyes, holding everything that had transpired the last month in an ocean of peace. A tear rolled down my cheek at the same time that a smile spread wide across my face. I turned to my journal and wrote:

I am a Warrior for Love.

Chapter 16—The Birth of a Warrior

> ***"Ease of Discipline"***
> *There is something beyond this.*
> *An ease of practice, of discipline.*
> *Where air floats all around.*
> *Open spaces in my lungs get filled.*
> *Don't tell me where the meadow is.*
> *Hold my hand and lie with me in this grass.*
> *Here, now.*

The Discipline

It was going to take more than a declaration, I knew. I also knew it was going to take more than a weekend workshop; more than completion; more than new projects; more than a budding partnership with my inner child; and more than a renewed romantic connection. I knew it would not come about from a magic moment, although there might be some along the way. No, this was going to require discipline and patience. Transforming my relationship to love was going to take everything I had. It was going to take every ounce of strength I possessed, even the strength I did not yet know how to access at that time. But I also knew that I was ready. I was committed at a level I could not articulate or fully understand. There was simply no other way forward that I would allow.

I set my feet firmly on the floor in front of the chair I was sitting on, pulled myself up to a tall seat, slowly picked up my pen, turned to my journal on the table in front of me, and wrote:

"To be a warrior"
Quiet presence
Strength
Patience
Slow rising
Passionate conversations in dark taverns
New possibilities
Integrity
Preparing for battle
Shedding
Letting go

I paused for a moment as I felt something sink into place, and continued:

Warrior for Love
Six-months training
Letting Go

"I am in training," I thought. "What do I need to let go of to cultivate the being of a warrior for love?" I brought my pen back to the page:

- I am letting go of attachment.
- I am letting go of people-pleasing.
- I am letting go of being reasonable and predictable.
- I am letting go of smooth sailing.
- I am letting go of coping mechanisms.
- I am letting go of being a victim.
- I am letting go of playing small.
- I am letting go of slouching.
- I am letting go of bingeing.

Chapter 16

- I am letting go of being sedentary.
- I am letting go of indecision.
- I am letting go of mediocrity.
- I am letting go of needing approval.
- I am letting go of who I thought I was to become who I really am.

I reviewed my list and began writing. Slowly, methodically, I wrote an entire page of lines for each item I was committing to let go of over the next six months. For each one I described the way it currently showed up in my life and its cost, and then wrote ten identical lines declaring my commitment to let it go. An hour passed; then two; and then three. I did not stop. My shoulders did not slouch. My feet did not leave their grounded place on the floor. Line after line my pen moved up and down and back and forth, my hand finding its rhythm, my mind ignoring the cramping in my fingers and the aching in my wrist that had begun spreading up my arm. I pressed on, until arriving at the last sentence for the last item on my list. I took a deep breath and wrote for the tenth time:

I am committed to letting go of who I thought I was to become who I really am.

The next morning while sitting with a cup of coffee and my journal on the balcony, I made it official:

Today, I am born a warrior for love.
I am still unfolding like a butterfly.
I am vulnerable and exposed.
I could be stepped on or dismissed.
I can never again be broken.

I Am Enough

I now live by the warrior's code.
I create from love.

The Storm

My heart was racing at a fever pitch as I rushed into the hotel room, made a bee line for a clear patch of floor and dropped my bags, half taking off my coat while scrambling to open my suitcase and pull out my laptop.

"Hi! Do you know what the hotel's internet password is?" I asked in a flow of words as I powered up my computer.

"Crazy day," I continued as I rushed over to the bed where Steph was sitting with an amused look on her face, for a quick hello hug.

She introduced me to her friend who was sitting on the bed opposite as I made my way back to my pile on the floor, internet password in hand.

"Nice to meet you. Just gotta finish this," I mumbled as my roommates went back to their conversation and I settled in cross-legged on the floor, laptop on my knees, and dove in. After about twenty minutes of typing I sat back to review the document I had been working on, took a breath, and glanced over at my phone. It was a little after 10:30 p.m. My heart picked up its pace.

"Oh no!" I thought. "Will I make it?"

It was Friday, June 5, 2015, and I was on a mission. I was in Seattle for the June AC program weekend and I needed three new clients papered and paid by 9:00 a.m. the next morning or I wouldn't be in integrity with the requirements of my contract as a mentor coach. That would require me to spend the day outside in the hall cold calling potential clients until I got hired. The thought of that possibility was revolting to me. I

Chapter 16

would not let it happen. I moved my work into the hallway so my roommates could sleep before turning back to the email I was composing. I completed it, attached the contract I had just created, pushed send, and then picked up my phone and began to tie up all the other loose ends.

After a few text conversations and one midnight phone call—to change the terms of a contract with a new client to ensure they complied with my coaching program requirements—I was starting to think I just might pull it off. A little over two hours later, I put down my phone for the last time. I'd done it! Two out of three new contracts were in my inbox; I had money in the bank from one new client; and firm promises from the others that the outstanding contracts and payments would be in my email and bank account by 9:00 a.m. the next morning.

I looked back at the text conversations on my phone and confirmed one last time that all was in order before closing down my electronics and sneaking back into my hotel room. A sudden wave of anger rushed over me and for a second my eyes filled with hot tears as they registered what time it was—1:15 a.m. I had to be up in less than five hours! I took a deep breath, pushed the emotion away, and began getting ready for bed, shaking my head and giggling instead at the insanity of my day before letting my exhaustion take over and drifting off to sleep.

The weekend went off without a hitch. My contracts and payments came in and I was able to be in the room to help the other leaders put on the program for the participants. I was congratulated for successfully generating three clients in approximately twelve hours the day before a program weekend, and, riding the wave of energy from that accomplishment, I didn't even feel tired despite my lack of sleep.

In many ways that Friday was a miniature replica of my last two months. Ever since I had generated a beautiful new vision for myself, I had set myself to work trying really hard to make a dent in its achievement. In the past three weeks, I had taken tremendous amounts of action. I had completed a public wholeness challenge, generating one vulnerable video every day for ten days and uploading it to my YouTube channel. I had written over 40,000 words of my book, completed the manuscript, and sent it to my editor for editing (something I had been trying to get done for over a year). I had taken on a few health challenges including an intense five-day cleanse, and meditating for fifteen minutes every morning and every evening before bed. I had followed tight daily schedules in a way I hadn't since working at my law firm and building up TYS. I had continued consistently publishing my daily poems. I had made daily posts on our AC leader team blog updating the status of my own projects and stating whether I was in integrity with the declarations I'd made and the milestones I intended to hit. And to top it all off, I had given myself high stakes rewards and consequences for all of my actions, buying myself presents that I would have to give away if I failed to do what I said I would on a particular day or by a certain deadline.

My flurry of action culminated in the generation of three full-pay coaching clients in less than one day—something I had never done before in the span of a month or a week, never mind one afternoon and evening.

On the one hand, I'd had incredible success in moving my projects forward. On the other hand, I was exhausted. I'd got caught up in the adrenaline. This was not how I wanted my projects to be going. This was not how I wanted to live my life. I thought back to the beautiful ceremony I had created only a few days earlier. This way of generating results was not in alignment with the deep shift I had committed to creating in how I related to myself, others, and the world.

Chapter 16

The Confusion of How

Upon arriving back home from the weekend, I was shaken. Monday morning, curled up on a friend's couch in Vancouver, cup of coffee in hand, I couldn't believe how, only two days after committing to a new way of being, I'd got caught up in my old way of striving to getting stuff done. I'd reverted to the adrenaline I lived on in my articling days. I was frustrated with myself. I was also scared. Two of my three new clients had only signed on for one month. Which meant I would need to do this all over again by the beginning of July. I knew I couldn't. I wouldn't. I would have to do it differently. Only I didn't know how. It felt like I was frozen between two worlds and I couldn't access either.

My projects all came to a halt. My editor sent my manuscript back with her edits. I glanced at it then ignored it. One of my clients stopped showing up for his calls. I texted him and called him a few times, then gave up. Another of my clients told me on every call in June that she would not have enough money to continue coaching with me in July unless a miracle happened. We talked about it and tried to generate possibilities for her, but I did nothing to generate a new client for myself in case she could not come up with the money in July. I told myself to go for a run or to dance, but I didn't.

By mid-June, I still had no motivation and the fear that I would not have enough clients by my next coaching weekend was starting to creep into my bones. I gathered all of my courage and tried to rally my energy back to its normal level, or at least to a level that would enable me to take some steps toward generating a client. I did every single thing I knew to do to motivate myself to get myself into action—inspirational quotes, TED Talks, journaling, reviewing my vision. It didn't work. In fact, everything I used to find inspiring was making me angry. This was not like me.

I decided to rent a little tiny house as an office in Victoria; the beautiful little home of a friend who was on vacation. Called La Casita, it was about a half hour walk from where I was staying with Scott. Every day I made my way out there and tried to work. And I did have some drive. I was still doing all of my coaching calls and writing my daily poems, and sometimes I would make progress on the pitch I was working on for my application to be a speaker and share my philosophy of self-love at TEDx Victoria. But mostly, all I had energy for was reading up about spirituality and universal love in various books and articles I came across on the internet, and writing in my journal. I just didn't trust myself to take action on my projects in a way that wasn't based in striving for approval and trying really hard to get somewhere and fill some void I no longer wanted to have to fill.

I was still in action on my internal work. I was talking with Bay once a week for our coaching sessions. Despite the fact that I was feeling less and less engaged in coaching—it felt too analytical, keeping me in my head instead of trusting in my spiritual path, where I sensed I needed to be—Bay was allowing me to be where I was at in my process and I was still getting value from our sessions. Scott and I were having more and more conversations of a spiritual and philosophical nature, contemplating our life purposes and the paths we were on, and where we felt they were taking us. At one point he suggested that what I was going through was something of an initiation or a rite of passage; a necessary part of the transition to full responsibility and adulthood that has been lost in our culture. On some level that resonated. It felt like I was going through some kind of a painful death-like process that was ripping me

Chapter 16

from the comfort of everything I knew, and I had no idea what was on the other side.

One day after a particularly frustrating hour of trying and failing to make myself send out some messages offering sample coaching sessions, I had turned to my phone, intending to call a teammate for support. I had missed a call. My stomach flipped as I read the name; it was Ada. We hadn't spoken in over a month. We had had a few more calls after my dream in March, and then I had gotten into action mode and had put our skin-prickling conversations out of my mind. I put my phone to my ear to listen to her message.

"How are you, my dear?" Her voice was full of warmth. "Just checking in. Your aura has a dirty brown overlay—you are holding on to negative energies and insecurities. Let me know if you need anything. Sending love."

I called her back and she had comforted me, telling me that I was on the right path. My aura was a bright white energy under the brown, she had explained, which signified angelic qualities of purity and truth. I simply needed to let go of the old energies and insecurities I was holding onto; an energetic and spiritual kind of surrender. Again, on some level it resonated.

A few days later, on June 20, I was staring unproductively at the open TEDx application on my laptop screen when a book tucked away on a shelf in La Casita caught my eye. It was called *Warrior of the Light: A Manual* by Paulo Coelho. I went over to it, picked it up, sat down right there on the floor in front of the book shelf, and read it in one sitting. It spoke of the being I desperately wanted to cultivate in myself.

I could feel this book was important, and that I was moving forward with each of the conversations I was having and things I was reading in some way I could not consciously understand, but because the month was nearing its end I started to get really worried. I wasn't figuring this internal shift out fast enough. "How would I ever generate new clients? What if I missed the deadline for getting my edits back to my editor?" I decided to reach out to my mentor coach team.

I called a teammate who helped talk me through my circumstance and offered me another lens to look through. He reflected that it seemed like I had taken myself and what I want out of the equation of my life, and, therefore, my "what for" was not strong enough to overcome the resistance. I could see where he was coming from. I wanted to make this part of my journey all about the world. I wanted to be pure love and make my life all about helping other people without resenting them or having any of my own needs whatsoever. I wasn't transformed enough to do that yet, and so I was stuck.

I shared with my mentor coach team on our blog what I had realized and felt like I was making some kind of progress. But as I sat there a few hours later trying to process a way forward that still allowed me to be human, I realized something else. That lens was still just that, a lens. It wasn't the truth. It wasn't the right answer. It was just one story for how my life was going. And it was the same with every other lens I had been offered all month. Within seconds my blood was boiling. I was furious. I felt played by my own self. I was so sick of choosing other people's perspectives as truth, becoming who they thought I was or who I thought they wanted me to be. I didn't want to pick any old perspective anymore just simply because someone offered it to me. How could they know it was the right one for me? How could I?

In my frustrated state I decided to post a blog a day to my team, each one cheekily offering a different perspective through which I had analyzed what was going on for me and why I was stuck.

Chapter 16

Letting my frustration out in this way was satisfying for a few days, but a week later I simply felt defeated. By June 30, all five of my coaching clients (including the two who had signed up for the year-long course I had launched back in March) had either completed with me or couldn't pay me. I officially had zero clients and I wasn't in action to get any more. I had missed the application deadline for TEDx Victoria, my book edits were overdue, and I was running out of time to generate new clients. I really didn't know what to believe anymore. I felt like I was going crazy, and analyzing myself through coaching was only making it worse.

"All these different lenses are stupid," I thought. "Coaching is stupid. It's helped me to see my beliefs and patterns and to know I can choose something different, but I don't just want to choose something different for the sake of choosing something different. I want to know the truth. I want to know my truth."

"But how?"

The Voice of My Soul

Over the next few days, reality hit. Although I had started taking more actions to generate clients, I knew that, considering my internal resistance, my efforts were not likely to generate any results. I was constantly fighting off tears. I declared a breakdown and sent a panicked outreach to my team. And then, just when I thought I could not hold on any longer, I couldn't.

Sitting on the high-top wooden stool at La Casita, my entire body shook with a fury greater than I could hold. I let it come. The rage was immense, only I didn't feel pain like I typically did when I was angry. Usually my anger was really hatred directed at myself for not being good enough in some way.

This time it just flowed. It wasn't directed at me. I felt alive and powerful as the fury coursed through me and out. I could sense there was something arriving for me. And then I felt a message in the rage-filled energy.

"Stop," it whispered gently as it coursed through my bones.

"Stop," it repeated, more firmly and loudly.

"Stop," it continued, over and over until the resonance was shouting in every inch of my being.

"Stop! Stop! Stop! Just stop!"

It was my truth. My own truth straight from the core of my being. It was the truth of my soul. I intuitively picked up my pen and opened my journal.

"Please speak to me." I wrote.

The response came from a voice deeper inside me. It said, "I am speaking. It is you who is not listening."

I knew it was true. I wrote about how scared I was and asked for forgiveness. I made a vow in writing to listen. I relaxed instantly. The rage and anxiety that had been overtaking me was gone. I sat there for a few hours writing to my soul and writing my soul's responses as they came. The messages I received over and over again in various forms were to stop and listen.

I felt sensitive to life, the world, and myself in a way I never had before. As I walked home the breeze felt alive on my face; the cars passing by seemed louder; the birds in the trees above my head seemed to be speaking their songs right into my ears. When I got home, my body was still vibrating with energy. I shared with Scott what had happened. He was amazed and could tell I was still partly in the experience. He offered to make dinner and suggested I do whatever I needed to do to honour what was going on for me. I thanked him and let the energy coursing through me take over as I went to sit out on the balcony. It was pure bliss being this connected to myself and the world around me.

Chapter 16

Scott came out a little while later with a delicious meal prepared for us. I picked up my spoon and prepared to take a bite when the energy coursing through me again burst into a rage. Fierce anxiety gripped my heart. I did not know how to eat from love. Tears rolled down my cheeks. I put the spoon down and explained to Scott what was happening.

"Wow," he said, with a mix of amazement and love. I took a deep breath and tried again. It was the same. Every time I attempted to take a bite my whole body was overcome with anxiety and rage.

I sat there until the energy had subsided to a quiet hum, allowed myself to get as present in my body as I knew how, and as I brought the spoon to my lips the anxiety did not return. Slowly I took a small bite. The flavours were intense; the texture and temperature of each of the ingredients swirled boldly in my mouth, dancing down my throat into my stomach, making their presence known. It was as if the food was having a conversation with a deep part of me that I had lost touch with long ago. I could hear my body. I could hear the wisdom there.

I slowly took another bite. I could feel the edges of the anxiety returning. That was enough. My body didn't want any more food right then. I started crying again, but this time they were tears of joy at the power of what I was experiencing. I looked up at Scott and smiled through my tears with a mix of awe and fear. I could not believe this was happening.

I spent the majority of the next two days alone writing in my journal to my soul. Each thought I had and each action I took felt like part of some long-lost sacred conversation. Each meal was a ceremony. I'd had brief experiences of this nature before—I'd called them aha moments or serendipitous moments or full-bodied resonance or energetic connection—but they had never been of this magnitude. This was not a passing resonance of truth. This was my truth; my intuition; the wisdom of my soul. Although I had not resolved my circumstances, I felt at peace. I had found a way forward. I would no longer choose to do things against the voice of my soul.

Chapter 17—Surrender and Letting Go

Decision Drama

Ever since getting in touch with the voice of my soul, I knew on a more conscious level why I had lost all motivation: I needed to stop. I needed to stop at some deep level I didn't fully understand. But because I didn't fully understand it, I didn't fully trust it. After three or four days of deep blissful connection with my soul, the voices in my head began to take over. Doubt crept in.

"You can't just stop everything, Danielle. You made commitments to people. You made commitments to yourself. This is your pattern. You take on something new really excitedly, you get to a certain point where you realize it's the same as everything else you've tried and that the void is still there, and then you quit and go on to the next thing. Can't you do something differently this time? Can't you keep your promises? Can't you stick it out?"

I rallied my energy and on Wednesday, July 8, on a last minute whim, I headed down to Portland for the first few days of World Domination Summit (WDS) 2015. I knew there would be no better way to get inspired, meet new people, and generate some new clients.

As part of the interactive nature of WDS, participants are allowed to host their own meetups or workshops that other participants can attend. I decided to do that. I put together a description and posted my meetup on the message board: it was called Warrior for Love, an open discussion about radical self-love. Nine people showed up. I led the group by sharing my journey of self-love and the philosophy I'd come to believe in. Then I opened it up to the group for others to share their journeys and anything else they felt called to say. It was a beautiful few hours.

Two days later I was on a bus to Seattle for the July AC program weekend. Although I had met many new people, including a few who were interested in coaching with me, I still officially had zero clients. I knew I wasn't trying as hard as I could be. I thought back to the three clients I had generated in the span of twelve hours a little over a month ago. I just couldn't do it. I would not cold call people. I would not send out Facebook messages and emails asking for referrals and offering sample coaching sessions. I began to shut down.

By the time I arrived in Seattle every fibre of my being was screaming stop again. I was ready to quit. My mentor coach teammates tried to reason with me. They offered me support. They offered me reflections. They reminded me of my commitments. They reminded me they loved me. They reminded me of the two AC participants I was coaching and how much I loved them. They reminded me I could have a month's grace to refill my coaching practice and get back in integrity with the program requirements. I was so afraid to lose my own truth or to adopt someone else's reflection as my own truth that I couldn't let in anything they said. Finally, one of the leaders simply asked me to make a choice—in or out.

I went for a long walk as I struggled with my decision. I passed a sign offering psychic readings on the sidewalk and I decided to go in. The reading was vague and unhelpful. I hadn't really wanted her to tell me the answer anyway. I thought about calling Ada but couldn't bring myself to do it. I thought about calling Scott or a friend or my mom, and then didn't. I didn't want anyone else's advice or perspective. I knew I had to make

Chapter 17

this choice myself. I wandered some more, thinking about all the commitments I'd broken in the past.

"You uprooted your entire life only eight months ago," I reminded myself. "Do you really want to do that again?"

I decided to stay.

The next week, one of my WDS workshop attendees became a new client without any kind of cold calling or sales tactics on my part. He was really excited to start coaching and I was really excited to work with him. I started thinking maybe I could do this in a way that wasn't so exhausting. But a deeper part of me just didn't want to. Within a week I was again stopped.

The back and forth continued. When I was alone with myself for a few hours, I could hear my truth. It had never changed. "Just stop," it guided softly. "Let go. Surrender to this."

When I spoke to teammates or friends, I doubted myself. I told myself my survival mechanisms were probably just tricking me into quitting and playing out my pattern so they could get really excited about the next thing I would take on to fill the void.

By the last weekend in July, I still only had one client and was not doing enough to be generating any more. I had one week left before the next AC program weekend. I needed to make a decision and either get into massive action or choose to get out. I took the entire weekend for myself. I created two day-long ceremonies. The first day I spent in a sacred space I had fashioned in the attic of the friend's place I was house-sitting, getting in touch with all the different versions of myself and understanding what each of them wanted and why. The second day I spent the morning journaling in the attic and then went for a long bare-footed walk through the streets of Vancouver, down to the beach, and along the ocean until dusk.

By the end of the weekend I had realized that this decision I was struggling with so epically wasn't just about my coaching program. This was the letting go I had declared back at the beginning of June. This was about letting go of everything I had ever taken on from a place of not being good enough and trying to fill the void.

"I am letting go of who I thought I was to become who I really am."

I reminded myself of what I had written. I *did* need to stop. I did need to let go. I did need to surrender. I had known it wouldn't be easy. But it was what I had already chosen all along.

"Are you open to being enrolled in staying?" The calm powerful woman at the front of the room was looking me straight in the eyes, demanding an answer with a mix of authority and grace.

Although I already knew the answer, I paused, hoping for one second I might find a way for my truth to be different. It was no use.

"No." I replied with a quiet sureness, holding myself together, trying desperately to ignore the ache in my gut and the accelerated throbbing of my heart.

"Then you need to leave now."

I stood up from my seat at the table where my AC team had gathered for our morning meeting and began collecting my things. Everything was happening in slow motion. My limbs were numb to their movements; my mind ghost-like and wandering. I stacked my cell phone on top of my coffee mug on top of my note pad, on top of my journal, balancing everything and hoping it would somehow not fall. I could see only a blur of the silent faces of my teammates around me as I pushed my chair in and turned toward the door. I walked slowly, methodically putting one foot in front of the other, feeling ethereal like I wasn't really there but somewhere in space where

Chapter 17

each step that I took had me drifting off course. I stopped for my coat, my purse, and my suitcase, and got all of my things in order so I could carry them away. In my dream-like state I somehow made it to the door.

I opened the door and looked back into the hush of the room, wanting to scream I had changed my mind; I wasn't really through. Only I was unable to speak through the haze of my internal world. No "I'm sorry," no "Goodbye," no "I really love all of you" came out of me to be heard. On some level I knew that speaking would have been no use. Anything I could say, they already knew.

I stepped through the threshold and kept walking in a trance, out of the hotel lobby and into the sunlit street without turning my head for a second glance. My suitcase clicked noisily behind me at every crack in the sidewalk as I wandered the streets until I found a café. I ordered a coffee, sat down with my phone, and looked up the next bus that would take me away.

The shock held out for the three-hour trip home from Seattle and the bus ride to Steph's place in Vancouver. As I sat down on the bed in her spare room, my bags all around me, I woke up to what I'd done, fell into myself on the bed, and let the tears begin to flow. After an hour of deep grieving, I pulled my journal from my purse, opened it to a new page, and wrote.

Dear soul,
I just left my AC family. What is this all in service of, this heartbreak? I know I have chosen, but it doesn't seem fair or right that I have to make such hard choices. I feel some doubt and so much fear. Why would I leave something so good? Can't I learn about love any other way?

Heartbreak All Around

"Will you?"
Will you allow me?
Will you allow my love?
Will you allow yourself to hear the music in your heart?
Will you allow the song of our hearts joining to be heartbreakingly beautiful?
Will you allow yourself to sink into the depths of your soul, look into my eyes, and allow your life to be altered forever?
Will you allow yourself to be with this earth-shattering sensation?
Will you allow me to reach you, to see you, to rock you at the core?
Will you allow my touch to be fire, my voice to be music, my love to be divine?
Will you allow your body, mind, heart, and soul to ache for me?
Will you allow the power of our love to drown out all time, all problems, all insecurity?
Will you allow our love to wake us from our slumber and, eyes finally open, be alive?
Will you allow yourself to be the one for me and me the one for you?
Will you allow me?

I had desperately wanted something or someone to be my everything.

On July 18, Scott left to attend a conference in France and then to walk the Camino de Santiago in Spain. He wouldn't be returning until September. I had known that his leaving was coming for over a month. I had even encouraged him to go as

Chapter 17

I could sense it was where he needed to be on his path. The day after he left I had been miserable. I knew the heartbreak I was feeling was partly because I would miss him, but mostly it was because before he had left we had had a long tear-filled conversation in which he had shared that he felt he needed some space from me and our relationship while he was away to really go deep into the journey he was embarking on. I understood. But I also knew that his needing space was more than just about his spiritual exploration. Despite the fact that we had worked things out in May and he had chosen to commit, all of our old issues were still there. I still felt like he had one foot out the door, and he still felt like I was attached. There was still an unhealthy power dynamic in our relationship. We both knew on some level that if our relationship continued when he returned, it would not be the same as before. We planned to talk very little while he was away.

After a couple of days of tears, I found the strength to trust that we would work it out when he got back, and that whatever that looked like would be for the best. I shut the door to the pain in my heart.

Between trying to make a decision about whether to leave AC and trying to figure out what I would do when my living arrangements ran out at the end of July, I hadn't left any time to dwell on my relationship and the question mark that it had become.

The living arrangements I ultimately made were to visit my family in Manitoba for the month of August. On August 4, two days after leaving my coaching program, fully feeling the impact of my leaving, and once again painfully aware of the uncertainty in my relationship, I arrived at my sister's place in Manitoba. I was heartbroken and exhausted to the point of defeat. I desperately wanted to enjoy my time with my family, but it was a battle to stay present and even more challenging to access any emotion other than despair. I curled up with my journal the day after arriving and tried to process what I was experiencing in writing.

Dear soul,
   I feel disconnected from everything, unable to enjoy the simple daily pleasures of life. Those daily things—food, conversation, games—I only use to drown out the incessant struggle in my mind, the growing desperation, the urgent sorting of stories, options, paths, solutions. Most of all, I use them to ignore the greatest killer of all, resignation, and pretend like it's not spreading like wildfire.
   I feel my fire fighting for its life; my mind stamping out embers with its chatter. "Please quiet now," I say as I pour myself a beer, as I watch the TV, as I engage in conversation with my sister about everyday things, as I try to be present; I try to care. I feel my embers dying, one coal snuffed out at a time leaving in their place a cold emptiness, a vast winter plain.
   "At least it will be quiet there," I think. I could stop caring so much, stop feeling this heartbreak over and over every time I realize my carefully laid plans will not do the trick, every time I leave yet again, my bags never fully unpacked in the first place.
   "You knew all along," a voice says. "Why did you fall in love so? Why did you let yourself get caught up in the feeling? Enamoured even, you were. Why do you burn so, only to stomp out your own flame time and time again, the fire never quite big enough, never quite strong enough, to hold through the waves of destruction? And then you go cold like this?"
   I am terrified of choosing a way forward. I don't know if my spirit can take another beating of this nature. One of these times the light will not return; all coals snuffed out, doused with sopping heartbreak. There will be a last time. I will become cynical at this rate, depressed

Chapter 17

even, suicidal perhaps. I am not afraid of death. I understand its appeal in these moments of bleak skies that seem to last forever. Do I really care what happens to the world? To others? To me? Do I really care what my purpose is? Would it not be a kindness if I could end all this agony, all this unfulfilled longing?

I feel I hold the pain of the world in my hand. The weight of that responsibility is too great. I fear I cannot do anything that would make a meaningful difference. And who am I to make a difference anyway, or to even think that my task could be so great? My ego would love it for sure. I am not sure my heart is up to the task.

What do you say, my soul? How do I go on? I don't know how it could be helpful to throw myself into the next thing. What am I training for? Do I actually get to help save the world? Do I get to decide? Does my heart have to break a million more times if I say yes? Am I strong enough to survive?

My sister thinks I'm crazy. It's so hard to communicate with her. We don't see eye to eye. Why can't I just be normal?

Although my writing did not solve anything, it did provide me with some measure of peace. Over the next few days at my sister's, and the two weeks at my childhood farm with my parents and my little brother after that, my writing to my soul intensified. My journal became my solace; my place to process the heartbreak, to accept the letting go, to surrender to this path I was on, and to maintain a shred of faith big enough to not let the darkness take over completely.

There were moments of joy and play with my family between the dark clouds, and I sometimes had the awareness of where I was on my journey, but mostly my inner world was stormy. I was in the middle of the most-expansive, all-consuming heartbreak I had ever experienced and it felt awful. When I allowed myself to be present in my body, my insides felt like they were being pulverized. I was not dying in the physical way we most often think about death, but in a very real way I was dying. I was experiencing a death of my deepest, most pervasive belief system; my entire way of relating to myself, others, and the world. It was the death of not being good enough and needing to fill that void from the outside in. Letting go of it was terrifying.

I didn't know another way to operate except to find the next thing and get really excited about it being the thing that would finally fill the void. I didn't know how to be myself from a place of already being full, and I certainly didn't know how to have relationships, how to create things, or how to love from that place. All I knew was that I couldn't do it the old way. No matter how much pain I had to go through to get to the other side, I was not willing to go back. And so I had to continue with this; this letting go, of everything.

By mid-August, I had let go of a lot of things.

Except for the one new client I had started with in July, I had let go of my coaching practice and everything related to it. I had completed with all my old clients and I had stopped trying to get new clients. (I had nearly referred my one remaining client to a new coach and cut myself loose completely, but I had had enough faith in myself and in how coaching works to know that if I was doing deep transformative soul work—and there was no doubt that I was—my client would get the benefit of that transformation as well. I was really enjoying working with him, and being inspired by his dreams and fast-paced transformation and he was getting a lot from the coaching. I decided to trust we had crossed paths for a reason and continued with our sessions, which were scheduled to continue until the end of the year.)

I had let go of applying to speak at TEDx Victoria. I had run

Chapter 17

out of temporary homes. I had stopped editing my book. I had quit being a mentor coach. I had left my AC team. Scott and I had stopped living together and had put a question mark on renewing our relationship. And now, although I really didn't want to, I knew it was time to let go of that question mark too.

"I hate you. I hate you."

My fingers pounded the keys with vehemence, as if it was my laptop's fault I was in so much pain. But my laptop was a mere casualty of my firestorm of hatred, not the source. I was letting go of Scott and had taken on a completion exercise to help me through it. It was excruciating but I knew I had to do it. There really was a power dynamic in our relationship. I was always trying to make it work. He was always leaving. And I was always blaming myself for his leaving and trying harder to make him stay. So far my efforts had worked, barely. He had always come back, and even now, he hadn't left completely. But this wasn't how I wanted a relationship to go. More importantly, this wasn't how I wanted to *be* in a relationship—always worrying my partner didn't want to be there, at least not as much as I did. I knew I deserved more. I knew I wanted more. I wanted someone to choose me completely. I wanted commitment. I wanted devotion and partnership. This wasn't it. I had been lying to myself. Our dynamic was not healthy for me. This had to end, no matter how much I loved him, and I did. Not since falling in love for the first time when I was sixteen had I loved someone so completely. And now that it was ending, I was feeling the opposite emotions to an equal extreme.

I was in a trance, typing madly letter after letter, sentence after sentence, page after page, the same three words over and over—"I hate you. I hate you. I hate you."—completely oblivious to everything; wearing the white lettering off my keyboard with the force.

When I finally paused about an hour in and blinked the tears that had been streaming from my eyes, there was still pain.

"The person I should really be angry at is myself," I thought. "For trying so hard to prove I was good enough. For letting myself again and again feel rejected. For allowing my self-worth to be contingent on his wanting me, and on our relationship being everything I had thought it was and wanted it to be."

But I couldn't get past the heartbreak to take responsibility for my own part. All I felt was hatred toward the man whom I had loved so much. I turned back to the keys; to the healing release of my rage-filled words.

I broke up with Scott by email that night. I no longer wanted the relationship we had had, and I no longer wanted to wait for him to come back in the hope he would suddenly be ready to commit and choose me fully. I could not hold on any longer. Holding on in this disempowered way had been killing me. I needed out.

The next day my completion continued. Once I had got all the rage out, I began to take responsibility for how I had shown up in our relationship. I knew to some degree I had been deeply attached to Scott being the one for me and deeply attached to our life together being the magical, beautiful thing that would finally fill my void. I could see that I had been trying to transform and heal myself and to transform and heal him so that we could get rid of the power dynamic and it could work. I had been trying to force him to open his heart. I had been trying to force myself to be more powerful in our dynamic. I had put a lot of pressure on myself, him, and our relationship. On some level I knew that our souls had been joined together for a reason, and that it wasn't necessarily for long-term partnership. My soul had chosen all of this, even the pain; especially the pain. It had all been necessary to fulfill the mission of transformation I had set myself on. I had grown so much through our relationship.

On the third day, I began to feel grateful. I felt grateful that I had allowed myself to feel my emotions. I felt grateful for all of this awareness, and for all that I had learned from our relationship. I thought of all the beautiful times we had shared—laughing at the constant stalling of his old van, Baby Blue; wondering about the Universe over beers as we stared up at the stars; dancing in the kitchen as we prepared a delicious meal; debating theories and ideas about life; coaching each other though challenges; sharing the experiences we were having on our path; giving in to the passionate fire of our chemistry; and curling up in each other's arms for hours without any sense of time.

Scott had given me the gift of a love powerful enough for me to have been willing to risk annihilating heartbreak. That love was a catalyst that had enabled me to find within myself the strength to let go of everything. The strength to let go of trying to be someone I am not, so I could allow myself to be who I really am. A mix of gratitude and grief poured from my heart and tears streamed down my face as I allowed myself to begin to let him go.

The Last Stand for Striving

For the remainder of my time in Manitoba, between my slowly easing grief and increasing moments of joy and love with my family, I began to face another familiar foe: confusion. If I wasn't a lawyer and I wasn't a coach, and I didn't have a home or a partner, who was I? And where was I meant to be? What did it mean to be a warrior for love?

My mind had no shortage of ideas. I needed a pilgrimage. I needed solitude. I needed a physical challenge. I needed a writing retreat. A pilgrimage of pilgrimages. I would climb Mount Kilimanjaro and then go on a two-week Ayurvedic retreat and then a one-week writing retreat. I might fast. I might need more solitude still. I was a poet. I had been consistently writing a poem every week day for the whole year. I could find a little hut somewhere and go deeper. I needed to write more books. I had so many ideas. I would finish the book I was working on. If I dedicated myself completely, I could write many more in the next year. Then there was my spiritual side. I was still talking to Ada regularly about my increasing energetic and empathic experiences and how we might heal the world with love. I was having more and more dreams and supernatural experiences. I needed to help people somehow. I should keep coaching and just allow it to become more flexible and healing in nature. I needed to share my philosophy of love. I needed to use my voice. I would start a weekly online video series or podcast.

Being without a sense of identity was torture. I needed a vision. I needed a belief system to live within. I was living in chaos. I had to pick something. And so I tried. I tried to will myself from an empowered place to choose one thing or idea as mine, and to get excited about it. I started planning a pilgrimage but never booked it. I forced myself to finish my book edits and sent them off to my editor, then felt queasy for the rest of the evening. I came up with outlines for seven more books then ignored them. I came up with a new vision for healing work with individual clients, but it felt wrong even as I was writing

Chapter 17

it. I thought about reviving TYS even though I knew I really didn't want to. I came up with more ideas. They faded fast. No matter how hard I tried to convince myself, nothing would stick. None of my new things lasted more than a few days or weeks at most. Despite my herculean effort to keep my old strategy alive, it would no longer work; I could not force myself to get excited about the next magical thing.

I also needed to make some money soon and I still had no motivation to rebuild my coaching practice. Every time I thought about calling someone to enroll them in coaching, putting on an event to talk about coaching, or taking any kind of action to generate clients, I became physically exhausted. Any other business idea I came up with generated the same kind of response. I was not ready to build something from my new way of being. I hadn't yet fully let go of my old business dreams and I knew I couldn't rebuild from a different place until I had.

There was a growing feeling in my gut that I had been ignoring: I wasn't done with being a lawyer yet. I had quit in a whirlwind thinking I had found the new thing that would make my life whole. I had left thinking I had found a better, more meaningful path; as if law were just not good enough. My leaving carried a hint of arrogance that I needed to renounce. On top of that I missed having a place to go to work every day where people challenged me, accepted all my weird quirks, and made me laugh. And if I was really honest with myself, a part of me missed the work itself. My mind loved the challenge of solving complex legal problems. After a few weeks I could no longer ignore it. I knew the deepest part of me needed to go back. I reached out to Jamie to set up a time we could talk.

My first night back in Vancouver, I stayed with Steph and we caught up over a meal and a glass of wine. We were both in a place of letting go. She suggested we hold a funeral for all of our fatally wounded and lifeless dreams. I was in. As we sat there colouring and reminiscing about all the people we had loved and the things we thought we'd be, laughing into the love of good friendship, I began to notice a warmth creeping in that I hadn't felt in a while.

Hours later, after ceremoniously burning our artwork, I stood alone staring out over the ocean at the starlit sky, cradling my mason jar urn. I said a prayer of forgiveness and released the ashes of my dreams into the waves as they lapped against the shore. I sat on a rock with my journal and wrote one poem, and then another until I had finally let my lifeless dreams go. Tears rimming my eyes, I looked up into the breeze as it swept a strand of my hair across my cheek. "Home." I whispered into the night. "I am going home."

A few days later I visited Jamie. After catching up on what had been going on in my life and his since last time I had visited a month earlier, I asked if KCM might be willing to take me back. Graciously, amidst a few jokes, he replied that so long as I was willing to make some kind of commitment, they would love to have me back. I thanked him and agreed I would send him an email with a proposed start date and my promise of commitment.

As much as I knew it was the right choice for me and as grateful as I was that my law firm was willing to take me back, when I left Jamie's office that afternoon in late August, a part of me was still fighting my return. I was afraid. Could I find a way to commit to law and not lose the spiritual path I was on and the sense of purpose I had found?

I knew I was devoted to living my philosophy of love, but it was so big. I felt I needed some kind of vehicle to carry it into the world, and law wasn't it. If I was going to work as

Chapter 17

a lawyer, I needed some other outlet for my spiritual work. I had faith, but I needed religion, I decided. And so, towards the end of August I began a process of trying to convert myself back to my childhood religion. I started reading the Bible. I attended services at a few local churches trying to find a good fit. I began writing to Jesus in my journal instead of to my soul. I prayed multiple times a day. I fasted for two days. I increased my conversations with Ada. I had a couple of pretty wild, supernatural experiences. I even thought about offering to pay for Ada's living expenses, or really anything she wanted, if she would devote her time to teaching me everything she knows. We could start a secret revolution together, I had thought. We would save the world. That would be something I would be willing to make money for, a worthy cause: the healing of the world. A quiet rational voice had been keeping me back from making the offer, but barely.

And then walking home from church shopping one morning I was hit with the truth: I was still striving.

"The whole idea I had of being on a spiritual path is inextricably tied to my ego's desire to be special," I thought. "I am trying to impress people spiritually, particularly Ada."

Just as I had been with everything else in my life, I had been relating to Ada and to "being on a spiritual path" as the things that would fill the void. I had become so attached to having some kind of special path that I was resisting having to take care of my basic human needs. I didn't want to need a job. I didn't want to need money. I didn't want to need a home or stability. I didn't want to need any of the material goods of this world. I wanted to be spiritually above all of that human stuff on some magical path where I would beam love at people and the Universe would simply take care of me. And if I had to have material goods, I wanted to have them for some spiritual good, not because I was actually a human and needed them myself.

The irony of it all was that my striving to be on a special spiritual path was preventing me from being at peace with working as a lawyer, and having a home and community, which was exactly what my soul had guided me towards. I needed to let go of this idea that spiritual life was separate from and superior to normal life, and that who I was and where I was at wasn't good enough. I was grateful for my conversations with Ada, and for all of the energies and dreams and other supernatural experiences that had allowed me to reconnect with my spiritual side. I now had my own way of connecting with that something universal and unseen, and I knew that that connection was something I would always have with me on my own path, no matter where I went. Even working as a lawyer.

"I don't need a church," I thought. "I just need to let go of this striving to be special."

That evening I went for a walk with the intention of walking down to the ocean to release my spiritual striving in the same way I had let go of my lifeless dreams. I made my way from Steph's place down to the water and tried to create some kind of ceremony of letting go. I couldn't get into it. I was restless. I turned away from the ocean and began walking. I had so much resistance. It felt like a war was being waged within me. It was as though the part of me that knew my own truth was trying desperately to break free of the chains my ego had placed on it. I was completely absorbed in the battle. Tears streamed down my face as I wandered aimlessly through the neighbourhood streets lined with impressive old homes and even more impressive, ancient trees.

"Why can't I just let go?" I sobbed to myself, soggy autumn

Chapter 17

leaves gurgling underfoot with each step. "This is not serving me. I am consuming myself, my spirit, my joy, and my love by trying so hard. I am killing myself by trying so hard."

A torrent of anguish flooded through me.

"Please God, Universe, soul, someone, anyone! Can you hear me?" I called into the night. "Please give me the strength to stop believing I am not good enough and to stop trying so hard to be something I am not."

Just then someone came up from behind me and jogged past me on my left, jolting me from my inner world. I was suddenly aware that I had been wailing, out loud, on a public street.

"This must be what it is like to go crazy," I thought. "I really am going crazy. I have broken myself down. Insanity has come for me."

I didn't know what else to do. Having released my striving as much as I knew how, I returned to my temporary home and got ready for bed. I was exhausted. I lay down to sleep and drifted off instantly.

Suddenly, I felt myself being lifted off the bed. I looked around. I was hovering. In the distance I could see a white light that was nearing. It grew bigger and bigger until it engulfed me. It was blinding. Someone was demanding I make a choice. I didn't know the question but somehow I knew the answer.

"Okay, I will feed the white horse," I said in utter defeat, years of layers falling to the floor. Instantly, to my right, dark clouds moved in and a whirlpool began swirling taking a dark black wolf down into its depths.

"Why is death drowning the black wolf?" I asked. The clouds shifted over the remaining light and everything became dark. I was falling, fast. I landed with a thud, drenched in sweat, adrenaline racing through my body.

I sat up and looked around me. My blankets had fallen off

me, but all the familiar contents of Steph's spare room were in their place.

"Had I really been lifted off the ground?" I wondered. It had felt so real. My hands were still trembling. I took a deep breath, reached for my journal, and wrote a few shaky notes. It felt like I was at a significant crossroads. I needed to make a choice. If I chose one way I would get sucked into the whirlpool. If I chose the other, there would be light. Although I was scared to let go, I knew that if I kept talking with Ada and kept trying to advance down this special spiritual path to save the world it would be out of a desire to be special; it wouldn't be from love. I might actually go insane. I needed to let it go.

Despite the late hour I called Ada. I sensed she would somehow know everything and would be awake to take my call. She was. I told her I needed space from her and the spiritual path we had been embarking on together so that I could learn to listen to and trust fully my own truth, and my own path. She understood. She said that right now my aura was primarily a rich green: a comfortable, healthy colour of nature that represents both growth and balance, and most importantly, leads to love.

"It means you are growing into both a healer and a centred person," she said. "I believe our work together is done."

"Thank you," I said. "For everything."

There were tears streaming down my face as I hung up the phone. Although I was grieving, I was peaceful. Just as I had in my dream, I felt years lighter. I had finally let go.

Chapter 18—Death of a Journey

"I'm not good enough and that's okay." The thought thundered through my bones leaving my skin rattling like delicate stacks of china after the rumblings of a mild earthquake. I stopped running. "I'm not good enough and that's okay!" I wanted to shout it from every roof top. "Not only that," my resonating earthquake continued, "I'm less than not good enough. I am absolutely nothing. Completely insignificant. Not even worthy of the judgment of good enough or not good enough. I am nothing. And that's okay too!"

A gleeful laugh escaped my lips as I basked in the irony of my truth. "I am nothing!" I shouted out over the ocean. "Nothing!" I threw my hands in the air and laughed again. "Nothing! Nothing! Nothing!" I did a little twirl and a jump and smiled into the first streaks of the rising sun.

It was the break of dawn, October 26, 2015, my last full day in Victoria, and I was out for an early morning run. Tomorrow I would be returning to Vancouver for good. The night before as I sat watching a YouTube video called "The Heart Can Bear It All" by Gangaji, it had felt like the final corner of a weight had lifted from my heart. I had been moved to tears, but I hadn't quite understood why. This morning I got it, and for the first time, to the very core of my being, I was ready for what was next. I was ready to go home.

I put my hands over my heart in prayer and whispered, "Thank you," and with a skip in my step I began to reflect on my life in Victoria over the past two months. My time here had been exactly what I had needed. Although by early September I had done some significant work to let go of my old striving ways, and I had known I wasn't going to jump into the next something new, I still hadn't felt quite ready to interact with my old world in a new way. I was scared I would slip back. I was craving a quiet space away from the world where I could strengthen my new way of being. An opportunity arose which offered me just that, and also to repay the kindness of a friend. My mentor from Victoria, who had given Scott and me a place to live for a few months earlier in the year, had sustained an injury. I offered to help out as she recovered.

By necessity, most of September and October became a time of slowing down and tending to daily life. We sat down and ate together at meal times and I got into a habit of preparing and eating three healthy meals a day, something I had lost since developing an eating disorder in my late teens. I did dishes and laundry and went out for groceries. We ran errands, went for walks, and saw plays. We had good conversations about life and talked about the details of our days. It was a quiet, nourishing side of life I had forgotten about, almost completely.

My time in Victoria also came with plenty of space for healing, writing, and, much to my dismay, more letting go. Just before arriving in Victoria the second week of September, I had come to the realization that my online presence was also based in my old way of relating to the world. I needed to let my online identity go. I stopped publishing my daily poems on Facebook, disconnected myself from email and social media completely and committed to staying away for five weeks.

Around the same time, I also realized that the focus of my book entitled "Create a Life You Love in Law," then in its second round of edits, needed to go. What I had written was no longer my truth about how to create a life you love. Not only that, my current experience was that how to create a life you love is highly subjective, and mostly elusive. I had no business

Chapter 18

telling anyone else how to do it. I could no longer put my name to my book. Although I was frustrated at the lost hours I had invested and felt guilty about the effort my editor had already made, I knew I had to let it go. In early September I threw the whole thing out and started over, writing this book; telling my story in all its messy uncertainty.

I also knew I needed some stability if I wanted to recreate my life in Vancouver from this new place. I was exhausted with moving. As exciting and trust-building as this past year of house-sitting had been, it was time to let go of my nomadic adventure. I needed a home. I began searching for an apartment in Vancouver. A friend of mine was also looking for a place, and we decided to share the cost of renting a two-bedroom apartment in the Kitsilano neighbourhood. The market was tough, but after some searching we found a place that was available mid-October. He had already moved in. I would be joining him the next day.

And then there was more letting go, again. Scott had returned from his pilgrimage in Spain in late September and we had reconnected. It had felt different being with him. I felt stronger. I didn't feel attached to his being "the one" anymore. We were both still magnetically attracted to each other and wanted to be in each other's lives in some way. We had begun being intimate again, and experimenting with different structures for our relationship. At first it seemed to be going okay, but after a particularly painful interaction a few weekends earlier when my heart had broken all over again, I realized it was still the same. I had been tricking myself. There was still a power dynamic. Through the heartbreak I ended our relationship again.

The back-and-forth nature of my break up with Scott was a reflection of the way I had been relating to most things in my life. Each day was a confusing mix of stepping forward onto new ground and running backwards and clinging to old things. There were moments of presence so real that time stood still and nothing else mattered, shuffled in with times of tricking myself into thinking I was being honest with myself, realizing I wasn't, feeling the heartbreak and loss all over again, and finding myself back at square one. I reconnected with Ada and my spiritual path, only to let go again in a more painful way. After my five-week social media hiatus I started a new online video series, called "Truths about Life, Love, and How to Save the World." I thought I had started it from a new place of creating from being already full, but although I didn't really want to admit it quite yet, I knew I needed to end that too.

Doing life differently, I was realizing, required a level of presence, intention, and courage that was way beyond what was comfortable for me, but I was committed. I would do whatever it took. I would forgive myself every time I realized I had tricked myself into thinking I was doing something differently when I wasn't. And I would humble myself and admit I had tricked myself as many times as it took to truly let go. And so it went. The past two months had been my testing ground; a safe space to get really honest with myself and learn to hear my own truth. My honesty muscle was getting stronger I could feel it.

I started reading *Language of Emotion: What Your Feelings Are Trying to Tell You* by Karla McLean and began trusting my feelings more. I no longer wanted to avoid them; I was practising the art of listening to their wisdom. I was learning to channel my anger into a bright light around me to restore the boundaries I'd long since allowed to be devastated. I was trusting my grief to tell me when I needed to let go. I was listening to my shame to know when I had disrespected myself so I could bring myself back into integrity. I was trusting my anxiety to tell me when I wasn't being honest. I was listening to

Chapter 18

the call of my body, which was inviting me toward music and dance. I started attending a weekly 5Rhythms dance practice with a local group—a freestyle dance that invited me to get even more in touch with my body and my emotions. I was putting that deeper connection with myself into practice everywhere in my everyday life. I felt peaceful with all of my letting go. I could see how I had been compromising my boundaries and self-respect in many ways in all areas of my life. I didn't want that anymore. I felt strong.

And now, arriving home from my earth-shattering run, I understood where my strength was coming from. I had finally come face to face with the demon I had been grappling with all along. All of my searching and letting go, all of the ideas, the dreams, the people, the places, the creations, and the beliefs that I had grabbed onto and then let go of in a multitude of different ways along my journey—from the moment I had let go of fine, to this very point—had, ironically, been leading me to the simple truth: I *was* fine.

"I *am* fine." I smiled.

My quest had led me back to the very thing I had let go of at the beginning. Only this time my being fine was not sarcastic. I was not pretending. I did not mean it only at a level that was superficial. I was truly and deeply *fine* in every fibre of my being; every single part of me and my life was completely okay. And not only that, I knew there would never be a part of me that was not okay, ever again.

In the video I had been watching the night before, Gangaji, a healer and speaker, was inviting audience members to sink into feelings of not being good enough and of self-hate that they were experiencing in the moment. As they did, every one of them found themselves at the same place: a place that could hold even feelings of self-hate and fears of utter insignificance;

a place of being okay. It had resonated deeply I now realized because this was the exact journey I had been on—one of learning to be with whatever I was experiencing in the moment, and doing the healing necessary to expand my beliefs and my heart to be big enough to allow it to be okay. And then learning to be with whatever was beyond that, and then beyond that, over and over again in an outwardly expanding movement, slowly coming to a full 360-degree allowance of the experience of being human, and doing the healing necessary to allow that wholeness to be okay.

I had allowed myself to be and to experience every belief, way of being, emotion, judgment, and part of myself that I had feared was not okay, from utter failure, loss, arrogance, hatred, selfishness, and manipulation, to sheer brilliance, divinity, inspiration, joy, passion, and full-bodied love, and everything in between. I knew there would be more circumstances in the future that would challenge me to experience more aspects of life and myself, and to grow even more, but I also now knew that whatever arrived next would be okay.

This morning I had realized that even being with the fear of not being good enough, I was okay. And in that deep peace of being okay I had found the core of what I had been running from: insignificance; being with the excruciating possibility that I was absolutely nothing at all. This is what had been missing from my life: the void itself; the thing I had created a million different strategies to avoid. I no longer wanted a strategy. I didn't want to get anywhere. I wanted to live there. Right smack in the middle of the mystery, where life is equally beautiful and ugly, and anything goes.

"Yes," I thought. "I am, and always will be, just fine. I am enough."

Chapter 19—The Hero's Return

"The Final Hour"
In the final hour.
Will you open to my eyes?
I shall keep painting.

I wanted to call this chapter many different things: The Messy Way Forward; A Budding New Way; the Old is Not the Old; Finding Fertile Ground; Planting a Tree. "The Hero's Return" was initially not an option at all, until on one of my coaching calls with Bay, in the editing stage of this book, she suggested my story fitted the archetype of the Hero's Journey. On some level, that felt true. I had felt a calling from deep within and had embarked on an epic quest with challenges and mentors and supernatural help. Now I was returning home to bring what I had learned into my old life.

But that's not why I chose this title. For the most part, my return did not feel glamorous or heroic at all. I called it the Hero's Return because I was realizing as I wrote the last chapters of this book that it was in embracing the messy ordinariness, the uncertainty of a budding new way, and the old that had become mine again in a completely new way, that I had finally found the courage to stand in fertile ground and plant myself a tree. I had become the hero of my own story, embracing all the parts of who I am, and settling in as myself.

This is how my heroic, human return went.

After that pivotal moment in October when I accepted at a core level the truth that I am enough exactly as I am, my life continued on right where it had left off. Although the occasions were fewer and farther between, I still caught myself running back to old things, and there were still more ways I needed to let go. It was a messy way forward filled with massive uncertainty. I knew I still wanted to build a business through which I would share my philosophy of love, but I had no idea what that would look like or when I would be ready to create a business from this new space. I knew I needed a solid foundation if I wanted to be able to do it, and so I dedicated November and December to creating that fertile ground. I began examining every single thing in my life with two questions: "Does this nourish me? Do I absolutely love it?" When the answers were no, I let it go; even the little things. I knew the tiniest thorn could take me out.

I purged all of my worldly possessions with those questions in mind, both in my apartment in Vancouver and my bedroom at my parents' farm in Manitoba when I went home for Christmas: old clothes and trinkets; letters, cards and mementos, including jewellery and a few gifts from my first love tucked away on a shelf in a box covered with dust in the closet of my old room. I purged my entire online presence deleting every video, post, quote, and photo I had shared in the past three years of building my blog and business. I deleted my entire Facebook, YouTube, and Instagram feeds from their inception. I took my website offline. I released everything that held old energy and created ceremonies to release my old attachments. And at the end of December I let go of my lingering ties to my coaching business, and completed with my last coaching client.

As I continued with my great purge, I also began slowly and intentionally bringing new beautiful things into my life and reinventing relationships with people from a different place: a budding space of deep honesty, self-respect, and pure desire; a space of being already loved and completely okay. I bought myself a new bed, duvet, duvet cover, and sheets. I bought myself new dishes and appliances. I received some new furniture from friends. I bought myself candles and made my new home beautiful and sacred. I bought myself new shoes. I bought myself new clothes. As if to help me out, the Universe had my laptop die. I bought myself a new laptop. I signed up for dance workshops and yoga that would nourish my body and soul. I continued on with the habits I had built in Victoria of making myself delicious meals and going for long walks. I intentionally reached out to friends I wanted to keep in my life and made an effort to be deeply honest with them. I reinvented my coaching relationship with Bay and signed on for another year with her.

I began work at my law office in mid-November 2015. I knew this would be the biggest test yet of my budding new way. Could I maintain boundaries around my personal time and space? Could I be honest with myself in the moment about when I needed a break instead of going for more coffee or chocolate and pushing through? Could I be present and take pride in my work without needing to make it my deepest passion? Could I make it sustainable and keep my commitment? Could I reinvent my relationship to law and show up from this new space?

For the most part my return to the legal profession has been wonderful. Every day I practise showing up at work more honestly than the last. I have not missed a dance or yoga class because of work. I have eaten well nearly every day. I have slept well nearly every night. I booked myself a writing retreat and continued making time to keep writing this book. I am enjoying the challenge of the work, and working with people I love and respect. Although in many ways my new life is the same as it was a few years back, everything is different. I am different, and, therefore, so is my life.

As I moved through each reinvention, the seed of the

new way that I had planted deepened its roots, and I found myself tackling more and more challenging situations and relationships. In late November my sister came to Vancouver to visit me. She had become engaged earlier in the year and I was to be her maid of honour. We decided to go wedding dress shopping with a couple of her friends who were also in town. We found the perfect dress. She looked absolutely radiant. And what was even more amazing was that all I felt was love. For the first time, not a single ounce of comparison clouded our relationship. Emotion welled up inside me and my eyes rimmed with tears. I couldn't believe my little sister was actually getting married. I was proud to be there with her and excited for her and the next chapter of life she was embarking on. Although we are different people and still don't understand each other completely, I am so grateful that we can be together as sisters, equals, and friends.

At home in Manitoba for two weeks over Christmas I began reflecting on the past few years. Though they had been among the most tumultuous of my entire life, they had also been the most nourishing, healing, and peaceful. I was present and enjoying my time at home with my family. I did not feel stressed to be in a familiar place where old habits ran deep. I did not feel the pull to overeat. I was consistently listening to my body and trusting it to tell me its needs. I was finding more and more courage to share honestly with my parents about the journey I had been on that was coming to a close and about what I was writing in this book. I felt deeply connected to my parents in a way I had never felt before, as equals and peers.

In late December, Scott and I reconnected and began a deeply honest conversation. We had both grown so much in the past few months apart. We each took responsibility for how our relationship had gone, acknowledged and apologized

Chapter 19

for the pain we had caused one another, and shared a mutual appreciation and desire for each other. After a few weeks of intimacy and connection, although there was no longer a power dynamic between us, he still did not want a long-term relationship, and I knew we could not continue being this close if I wanted to fall in love with someone new. We got to a place of unconditional honesty, and after a long walk and some tears, we parted ways. As I walked away into the cool of the night, my heart filled with gratitude and light. This time I had truly let go.

Toward the end of 2015, I had also begun to get glimpses of what might be next. I was starting to see that the seed I had planted was actually a tree, and that it had been growing this whole time. On New Year's Eve, Steph asked me what my intentions were for the New Year, and I answered without hesitation: creation from love, from a place of already being full.

"It feels like I am writing my life," I had continued. "I have just finished writing about this quest I have been on—I sent the manuscript to my editor yesterday—and I know I am embarking on another."

A few days later as I was walking home from work over the Granville Street Bridge my truth settled in a little deeper. "I get to write the quest and then I get to share the story," I thought. "I am writing my life to write my life."

I smile spread across my face. I stopped, stretched my arms wide and turned toward the sun that was streaking yellows and reds over the ocean, and whispered, "I am writing my life to write my life." I tilted my head to the sky as I began to laugh and spoke more boldly, "I am writing my life to write my life."

I Am Enough

Epilogue—The Answer to Why

I am writing my life to write my life.

The answer to the frustrating question why that tormented me on a Sunday evening in early January 2013 is as simple as this deceptively simple sentence: I am writing my life to write my life.

Three years ago when I set myself on a mission to answer the question why for everything in my life, on some level I knew in my core there was an answer; that there had to be a bigger reason, a deeper purpose for my life, and everything that I did.

And I was right. But what I hadn't realized then was that the moment I pushed send to cancel my run I was already living my answer. From that moment my life was infused with meaning; every single thing I did was guided by a deep soul-quenching commitment to my journey of discovery. I had taken the driver's seat in my life at a level deeper than my conscious mind could comprehend: I was writing my life.

Consciously I believed I was going somewhere, to some far off destination at the end of my mission where I would finally be peaceful and fulfilled. I did go to many places on my journey. I ventured into my internal beliefs, my emotions, my body, my spirituality, and my childhood. I explored relationships, careers, homes, lifestyles, and business ventures. I fell in love deeply and had my heart broken utterly many times. I tried on many new identities, beliefs, and paths I thought I would never have the courage to experience. I created and let go; created and let go; created and let go.

But my soul knew all along that where I was going was where I had always been, and where I couldn't not be. I was

Epilogue

not travelling to some distant land, but stripping myself of the layers of refuse that had collected over my own land—removing one by one the conditions I had placed on hearing my own truth and allowing myself to be me. I was coming home the whole time, not realizing I was already there.

When I was near the ending stages of writing this book, I stared out over the ocean and declared, "I am writing my life to write my life." Writing my life is really what I had been doing all along. Looking back over the messy process of writing this book, I can see the hard evidence of this answer.

Near the beginning of this journey, I turned an ear inward to begin to explore what I might be passionate about. I was flooded with visions of my first unfinished novel and my high school poem. I remembered I love to write. A few weeks later I undertook my first acts of creation: I dreamed up a mission and started a blog, one that would chronicle my journey. I was writing my life (dreaming up a vision and living it out) and writing my life (sharing my journey).

A few months in, an idea began to take hold, in whispers at first: I would one day write a book. By the end of one year of deconstructing the beliefs and conditions I placed on myself and on hearing my own truth, I knew without doubt I needed to write a book. I attended a workshop with Influence Publishing. I sketched out an idea: I would write a book to teach lawyers to trash their stress and create a life they love. I signed a publishing contract. I began writing. All the while I was still writing my life (dreaming up a vision and living it out) and writing my life (sharing my journey).

In 2014, as I continued to deconstruct my belief system and to remove even more of the conditions I placed on my myself and my own life, I began realizing the book I was writing was not quite right. I started again from a new angle: the latest strategy I had for creating a life I loved. All the while I was still writing my life (dreaming up a vision and living it out) and writing my life (sharing my journey).

In early 2015, I hit the next level of deconstructing my beliefs and the conditions on my life. My book again no longer resonated. I began writing a new version, this time quickly, so I could finish it before I changed my mind. I forced myself to finish my manuscript and sent it to my editor. All the while I was still writing my life (dreaming up a vision and living it out) and writing my life (sharing my journey).

In late 2015, I again came to the realization that the book I had written was not the one I was meant to write. My words no longer resonated as the truth I needed to share. And then I got it: I wasn't meant to tie up all the loose ends and offer an answer to the question "How do you create a life you love?" I was still living the journey myself, and I always will be. I was meant to do what I'd already been doing all along: write my life (share my journey).

I think on some level I had known from the beginning this would be the book I would write. I certainly had prepared for it. I had recorded my entire journey in detail over various mediums—my TYS blog; my coaching check ins; emails and Facebook messages with friends and teammates; my Facebook, Twitter, and Instagram feeds; my YouTube channel; my daily poems; my AC blog posts; and my journaling, which had intensified as my public blogging had slowed. I had captured every turn of my journey in all its messiness. It was a commitment that consciously I was unaware I had made; one that had risen out of some deep necessity. Writing was my mission's conjoined twin. It was not until I wrote out my experience in some form that I could move forward in my journey. One could not continue its life without the other.

Epilogue

The moment I emailed my editor in September to tell her that the book I had written was not the one I was meant to write and that I needed to instead share my journey, a tidal wave of words began pouring out of me. It was as if my story had simply been waiting for my permission to be told. I sat down and wrote over twenty thousand words, over the next forty-eight hours, completing a good chunk of the early part of this book. It felt incredible. As I moved along in the telling of my story the writing became slower, and I had to take more and more breaks to complete my processing of more recent events and to arrive at a place of being able to be the teller of the story, instead of the one still living it. But writing this story has never stopped feeling right.

The entire process of writing it I was engaging my *why*, my purpose, my destiny, my soul, my essence, my unique life force, or as one of my favourite contemporary poets David Whyte would say, my own unique conversation that I am invited to engage in in this life. That invitation to engage my purpose—my conversation—had always been there, only I had never been able to hear it because I had held so many conditions on listening to my own truth. I would only listen to my truth if it matched the ideas of success and being good enough that I gleaned from others and the external world. That I finally came to write this book is a result of me removing enough of my own limiting beliefs that I began to hear and trust in my own truth.

In the later stages of writing this book, as I began to accept at a soul level that I was enough, exactly as myself, my writing became a dance with my life. The more I surrendered to the process, the more I sank into a place of bliss. Process, write, let go, process, live, work, play, connect, feed myself, write, sleep, dance, process, let go again, cry, dance, laugh, write. Process. Write. Ecstasy. Write. Frustration. Write. Ecstasy. Joy. Exhaustion. Write. Ecstasy.

I Am Enough

Grace. The whole experience has been messy and sublime. I am living my conversation, every moment of my life infused with purpose, with dedication, with my deepest why.

I never expected living my purpose would look like this. I had no idea when I started on this journey that my starting was actually the answer I have been searching for all along. I would not have allowed it to be my truth in the beginning. I had had too many ideas of what success and my own identity looked like. I had been afraid of my own truth. But now it feels right. I feel my passion deep and powerful right here with me as I write, and a deeper more grounded commitment too—making me take breaks, sleep, do my legal work, enjoy relationships, engage in dance and yoga, allow space for the process, and keep other commitments to sustain me and carry me through.

I am engaged with all of it; holding all of it; not trying to get somewhere; living and embodying the journey as I write it. I feel more passion in my actions now than ever before, only it is a deeper kind of long-term passion; a knowing of who I am, and that I get to keep writing my life; living my purpose, my conversation, my why, forever.

I am writing my life. I am writing my life!

Epilogue

Author Biography

Danielle Rondeau is a writer, lawyer, poet, speaker, and coach. She is the author of the eBook *Trash Your Stress*, and the poetry book *Remembering Wholeness*. You can find out more about her books and other activities at www.daniellerondeau.com. She practises law at Killam Cordell Murray and lives in Vancouver, Canada, where you will find her dreaming up and living out her next adventure.

Speaking Engagements and Workshops

Danielle is a writer and teller of stories. Passionate and vulnerable in her speaking and writing, she shares her soul with humour, intelligence, and compassion. Her work spans a wide range of topics including overcoming addictions, reducing stress, cultivating deep self-love and acceptance, living our life's purpose, and exploring the depths of what it means to be human. She writes a blog at www.daniellerondeau.com/blog/ and has hosted workshops for lawyers, law students, writers, and entrepreneurs.

Danielle is available for select speaking engagements and workshops. You can contact her with inquiries at: Danielle@daniellerondeau.com.

Other Books by Danielle

Remembering Wholeness is a book of poems, raw, heart-wrenching expressions of what it means to be human in all the ways that we are.

Trash Your Stress is an e-Book collection of the best of the "Trash Your Stress" blog, offering stress-busting tips to stressed-out professionals.

Website

www.DanielleRondeau.com

Social Media

Facebook
www.facebook.com/Danielle-Rondeau-445323428875322/

Twitter:
www.twitter.com/RondeauDanielle
Instagram:
www.instagram.com/daniellelrondeau/
YouTube
www.youtube.com/channel/UCjckruZMXgZbwQRbUdgftng

If you want to get on the path to becoming a published author with Influence Publishing please go to www.InfluencePublishing.com

Inspiring books that influence change

More information on our other titles and how to submit your own proposal can be found at: www.InfluencePublishing.com

CPSIA information can be obtained at www.ICGtesting.com
Printed in the USA
LVOW08s2105290416

486009LV00002B/27/P